PEOPLE AND FOOD TOMORROW

Proceedings of The British Nutrition Foundation Conference on 'People and Food Tomorrow', held at Churchill College, Cambridge, 1–4 April, 1976

PEOPLE AND
FOOD TOMORROW

Edited by

DOROTHY HOLLINGSWORTH
Director-General

and

ELISABETH MORSE
Scientific Officer

The British Nutrition Foundation
London, England

APPLIED SCIENCE PUBLISHERS LTD
LONDON

APPLIED SCIENCE PUBLISHERS LTD
RIPPLE ROAD, BARKING, ESSEX, ENGLAND

ISBN: 0 85334 701 8

WITH 22 TABLES AND 9 ILLUSTRATIONS

© APPLIED SCIENCE PUBLISHERS LTD 1976

Composed by Eta Services (Typesetters) Ltd, Beccles, Suffolk
Printed in Great Britain by Galliard (Printers) Ltd, Great Yarmouth, Norfolk

Preface

At the first BNF Conference we considered the nutritional condition of people of different ages in Britain in 1973. The proceedings were published in a book which was aptly called *Nutritional Problems in a Changing World*. The second Conference was held in April 1976 when the world was changing even more rapidly. On this occasion we planned to take into consideration not only the scientific but also the economic, political and social factors affecting food supplies which are arising in the last quarter of the 20th century. We were particularly concerned that both industrialised and developing countries should be given due attention because in an increasingly shrinking world we will all have to face the same problems. The evidence suggests that as developing countries become more developed their aspirations are increasingly towards a Western way of life, which includes increased demand for commodities such as meat and high quality fats. We did not intend this Conference to be merely a discussion of potential food production, rather we wished to discuss the main constraints on adequate nourishment. The constraints include not only the physical limitations to the cultivation of land and water, but also the state of international relationships, the purchasing power of the individual and the social context in which technology must be developed and applied.

The various committees of the Foundation provided many suggestions for the programme of the Conference, but the Foundation is particularly indebted to the members of the conference planning committee from whom the final ideas for the structure and detail of the Conference evolved. They were Professor R. J. L. Allen, Dr K. L. Blaxter, Dr Sylvia J. Darke, Dr Magnus Pyke and the Officers of the Foundation: we met under the Chairmanship of Sir Frank Young, then President of the Foundation, who subsequently chaired the Conference with his customary skill, grace and humour.

The main programme did not include a session on the effects on British food supplies, or indeed on those of any other country, of British membership of the EEC. We were fortunate, therefore, in securing as our guest speaker at the conference dinner Mrs June R. E. Evans, OBE, a former Chairman of the Housewives' Trust, who is now a member of the economic and social committee of the EEC. She explained that on this committee are represented employers, trades unions and a miscellaneous group which includes the professions, small businesses, farmers and consumers. She stressed the fact that those members of the general public who often feel themselves to be distant from governments have, through this committee, a powerful voice. She stated that statutorily the economic and social committee has to be consulted on nearly all regulations on foods and she made a direct appeal for good, unbiased, expert help. Her informative and amusing account of the way directives on food are made in the EEC threw interesting light on an important aspect of the Conference's central theme, the problems involved in meeting the needs and wants of people for food in the foreseeable future.

Our task as editors of the conference proceedings has been made easy by the ready cooperation of all the speakers. We thank them for the speed with which they replied to our enquiries and responded to our requests.

We should also like to record our thanks to Mrs Evelyn Vittery, the Conference Organising Secretary, and to Miss Brenda Ewington, a member of the Foundation Staff, who acted as Assistant Organising Secretary, and who helped us to prepare the material for publication. Finally, we should like to express our especial thanks to Sir Frank Young for his guidance throughout and for steering the conference plans to a successful conclusion.

DOROTHY HOLLINGSWORTH
ELISABETH MORSE

Foreword

PROFESSOR SIR FRANK YOUNG, FRS

Chairman

The objectives of the British Nutrition Foundation include that of acting as a bridge in communication—between scientists of many disciplines concerned with nutrition and food; between those in industries concerned with the preparation and supply of food and university investigators; and between teachers of many different sorts and at many different levels who necessarily include the discussion of food and nutrition in their teaching. An important way in which the British Nutrition Foundation can help to fulfil this objective is by the arrangement of conferences at which matters of nutritional importance are discussed by contributors to those subjects which further the understanding of nutrition.

The First Research Conference of the British Nutrition Foundation was held in the spring of 1973, and was a great success. The papers read at that Conference were published later in a volume entitled *Nutritional Problems in a Changing World*. The fact that a large number of copies of that book were sold reveals that there has been an eager interest in the subjects that were then discussed.

The arrangements for the Second British Nutrition Foundation Conference began with the idea that this Conference should consider the problems which will arise during the rest of the present century in keeping the population of the British Isles properly fed in a changing world. The idea was that the Conference should particularly consider the problems of Great Britain. The view was taken that all parts of the world are now so mutually interdependent that discussion of problems as they affect the inhabitants of Britain cannot effectively be considered alone. They must be related to the probable future changes in the world as a whole— in economics, in the production of food, and in changes in population, during the last quarter of the 20th century.

At the Conference two special evening lectures were given: the first, the opening address, by Mr J. M. Goldsmith, was on the subject of 'Food quantity and quality', while the second, by Dr K. L. Blaxter, was on 'Agriculture and the provision of food in the People's Republic of China'.

In the first session, under the title 'Food requirements of people', the first paper underlined the great difficulty of predicting the numbers of

people who will need to be fed in Britain and elsewhere in the world
during the future years. This was discussed with special authority with
regard to India later in the same session. The second session, on 'Nutritional requirements and national policies', and the third on 'The provision
of food', gave rise to lively discussions and some interesting disagreements.
In the closing session, 'Constraints on meeting the needs and wants of
people', there was an emphasis on the need both for new knowledge
and for new attitudes to the employment of the existing knowledge.

The membership of the Conference included representatives of the
Nutrition Foundations of the Netherlands, Sweden, Switzerland, and the
United States, while those who took part in the Conference came from
12 different countries. The aim of the British Nutrition Foundation to
foster international cooperation in the consideration of the problems of
nutrition was materially aided by the presence of so many representatives
of different nationalities and of different disciplines and activities, both
industrial and non-industrial.

As was so with the First Conference, the papers and lectures are now
published in book form, this volume being under the editorship of Miss
Dorothy F. Hollingsworth, the Director-General of the British Nutrition
Foundation, and Miss Elisabeth Morse, the Foundation's Scientific
Officer. I believe that this book is in every way a worthy successor to the
first, and I hope and expect that a series of such books will appear over
the years to record the development of the immensely important subjects
with which the British Nutrition Foundation should and does concern
itself in an evolving world.

Contents

List of Contributors

K. L. BLAXTER, FRS
Director, The Rowett Research Institute, Bucksburn, Aberdeen AB2 9SB

W. BRASS
Professor of Medical Demography and Director of Centre for Overseas Population Studies, London School of Hygiene and Tropical Medicine, Keppel Street (Gower Street), London WC1E 7HT

J. B. M. COPPOCK, OBE
Honorary Visiting Professor, Surrey University and formerly Director of Research and Scientific Services, Spillers Limited, Old Change House, 4/6 Cannon Street, London EC4M 6XB

N. EEG-LARSEN
Professor, Department of Physiology and Biochemistry, Division of Dietary Research, Odontological Institute of Physiology and Biochemistry, University of Oslo, Løkkeveien 7, N—Oslo 2, Norway

J. M. GOLDSMITH
Chairman and Founder, Cavenham Limited Anglo Continental Investment and Finance Co. Ltd., 65/68 Leadenhall Street, London EC3

C. GOPALAN
Director General, Indian Council of Medical Research, Ansari Nagar, New Delhi—110016, India

GEORGE HOUSTON
Titular Professor, Department of Political Economy, Adam Smith Building, University of Glasgow, Glasgow G12 8RT

A. T. JAMES
Head of Division of Bio-Sciences, Unilever Research, Colworth/Welwyn Laboratory, Unilever Limited, Colworth House, Sharnbrook, Bedford MK44 1LQ

LEONARD JOY
Professor, The Institute of Development Studies at The University of Sussex, Andrew Cohen Building, Falmer, Brighton BN1 9RE

D. W. LARBEY
Unilever Research, Colworth/Welwyn Laboratory, Unilever Limited, Colworth House, Sharnbrook, Bedford MK44 1LQ

JOHN MCKENZIE
Head of Business and General Studies, the London College of Printing, and Director, Research for Management Limited, Suite 68, Kent House, 87 Regent Street, London W1R 7HF

J. MAURON
Head of Research Department, Nestlé Products Technical Assistance Co. Ltd., Case Postale 88, CH-1814 La Tour-de-Peilz, Switzerland

M. EGGEN ØGRIM
Leader of the Division of Dietary Research, Odontological Institute of Physiology and Biochemistry, University of Oslo, Løkkeveien 7, N—Oslo 2, Norway

H. C. PEREIRA, FRS
Chief Scientist, Ministry of Agriculture, Fisheries and Food, Whitehall Place, London SW1A 2HH

N. W. PIRIE, FRS
Visiting Professor, Department of Food Science, University of Reading, and formerly Head of Biochemistry Department, Rothamsted Experimental Station, Harpenden, Herts AL5 2JQ

A. S. TRUSWELL
Professor of Nutrition and Dietetics, Head of Department of Nutrition and Food Science, Queen Elizabeth College, Atkins Building, Campden Hill, London W8 7AH

R. G. WHITEHEAD
Director, MRC Dunn Nutrition Unit, Dunn Nutritional Laboratory, Milton Road, Cambridge CB4 1XJ

CHAPTER 1

Food quantity and quality

J. M. GOLDSMITH

Cavenham Limited, London

There are two major pressures on the supply of food: increasing world population and rising standards of living. The United Nations' 'medium' assumption is that, between 1970 and 1990, world population will grow from 3621 million people to 5346 million, an increase of more than 1700 million in just 20 years. That is the present, combined, population of Britain, France, Germany, Italy, the five other countries of the European Common Market, the USA, Canada, Australia, New Zealand, Eastern Europe and Russia, and even then there would be 728 million to spare! (FAO, 1974, Ministry of Agriculture, Fisheries and Food, 1974). These are the extra people we are supposed to be able to feed in 14 years' time, which is not a long time in terms of agriculture. And, according to the Food and Agriculture Organization of the United Nations (FAO), approximately 460 million people already have a diet below the minimum recommended for adequate protein and energy supply (FAO, 1974). FAO also estimates that, with no increase in current levels of income, there will be an increase in food demand of 50% in the 15 years between 1970 and 1985, but that, should world incomes rise in line with the UN forecasts, we will need 70% more food in that 15 year period. Like most forecasts, these will probably turn out to be wrong, but there is plenty of margin for error.

Certain countries are increasing their standards of living. As people grow richer they tend to consume more meat, and hence indirectly more grain. It takes an average cow 17 kg of vegetable protein to put on one kg of edible animal protein (Holmes, 1971). Thus, whereas in India, the average *per caput* consumption of grain is 158 kg per annum, in the USA it is 675 kg (Brown, 1974). Japan is an example of the switch to a meat diet as prosperity increases. Between 1960 and 1972, annual meat consumption increased from 6·4 kg per head to 23·3 kg, an increase of 264% during a period when incomes increased by 204% (Allaby, *et al.*, 1975). It has been estimated that of the recent 30 M tonnes (Mt) average annual growth in world grain output, approximately 22 Mt are absorbed by population growth and 8 Mt by rises in *per caput* incomes (Brown, 1974).

This has been known for a very long time and much has been done to anticipate it. During the late 1950s and early 1960s, a great world effort

1

was made to bring about the Green Revolution. The development of high-yielding wheat, maize and rice hybrids, usually called 'miracle strains', combined with the increased use of fertilisers, improved methods of irrigation and higher capital investment, resulted in a large increase in world food production. It seemed that modern technology yet again had overcome a major problem and that, in the process, it was creating a new one—world surpluses of food. To control this second problem, arable land was withdrawn from production and subsidies were paid so that it would remain fallow. In the USA, more than 20 M hectare (Mha) of arable land were treated in this way (US Department of Agriculture, 1974).

Then, in 1972, there was a reversal. Wheat production fell by 2·1%, coarse grain production by 2·8%, rice by 5%, and world fishery catches by 6·7% (FAO, 1974, 1975). As a result, our grain stocks became almost exhausted. Suddenly the world had become dependent on each year's harvest for next year's food. The margin for error had become perilously small.

Obviously, this led to a reappraisal. The standard plans that emerged were, as before, based on improved technology, bringing more land under the plough, higher capital investment, and all this on a world scale. Unfortunately, each of these elements seems to present some difficulties. Already, the technological innovations of the past are producing diminishing returns. In the UK, for example, arable yields per acre have ceased to grow in line with the use of fertiliser per acre. Eight times more nitrogen fertiliser is used now compared to the end of the war, and yields have increased by about 80% (Ministry of Agriculture, Fisheries and Food, 1968, and annually). In the USA, since 1950, there has been a 500% increase in the use of fertiliser and a doubling of yields (Lockeretz, et al., 1975). To raise yields of maize in the USA from 90 to 100 bushels/acre (2300–2500 kg) requires much larger quantities of nitrogen than was needed to raise yields from 50 to 60 bushels (1300 to 1500 kg). The increased use of fertiliser is also not without its problems. Highly soluble nitrate fertilisers are leached easily from soils into waterways. In still water they may cause eutrophication; in water abstracted for domestic supply they may constitute a health hazard. The total amount of nitrogen reaching surface waters in and around the UK from land drainage and from sewage effluent amounts to the equivalent of more than 40% of the fertiliser nitrogen that we use on our farms (Owen, 1973).

The continued development of 'miracle strains' also creates genetic vulnerability. Nature, in its generosity, gave us a system based on polyculture. There were thousands of genetically different strains of most of our crops. By developing strains with far higher yields, technology has encouraged the conversion of polyculture into monoculture. This is dangerous because crop susceptibility to attack from most diseases and some pests is transmitted genetically. Thus an attack that once might have affected one strain among many may now obliterate whole crops. There are some lessons to be learned from the setbacks experienced by monocultures in the 19th century, such as the potato blight in Ireland, which reduced the population from eight to four million, two million of whom died from starvation; or the Ceylon coffee rust, which eliminated all the coffee plantations in Ceylon and turned the British into a tea drinking nation. In 1946, Victoria blight severely damaged the USA midwestern oat crop. The recent epidemic of southern corn leaf blight reduced the US maize crop by 15%. Epidemics have annihilated the American chestnut and at present are destroying elms on both sides of the Atlantic. It was following the corn leaf blight that the National Academy of Sciences put in hand a general study to assess genetic vulnerability among a broad range of crop plants. The conclusion was not encouraging. It was that a whole range of important crops is now vulnerable (National Academy of Sciences, 1972).

 Bringing more land under the plough is not as easy as it sounds. The 20 Mha taken out of production in the US have now been brought back. Throughout the world, much of the land that appears suitable for agriculture is already under cultivation. What remains is mostly marginal land in tropical areas with thin, sometimes lateritic soils, which tend to deteriorate very rapidly once deprived of their tree cover. Though not tropical, the experience of Kazakhstan is eloquent. In the 1950s, this vast area of marginal land in the USSR was put to intensive agricultural use. In a few years its fertility was exhausted and yields tumbled.

 Soil deterioration is probably one of the greatest single problems that we face. It is a basic rule of nature that we obtain nothing for nothing, yet throughout history man has been unable to resist the temptation to take more than he returns. One need only look at North Africa, once the granary of the Roman Empire, to see what can happen. The Roman city of Thysdrus once had a coliseum which seated 65 000 spectators. Now it has been replaced by a poverty stricken village called El Jem, surrounded by desert. Similarly, the fertile crescent that once fed the civilisations of Sumeria and Babylonia are now no more than deserts, as are those parts of the Indus Valley that were the cradle of the first civilisations of the Indian subcontinent. We find it very difficult to learn from the past, yet today our population is so vast and our technology so effective that we can destroy thoroughly and overwhelmingly. Few things are more dangerous than an efficient, energetic and well equipped man who lacks wisdom. If he chooses the wrong road, he proceeds with terrible speed. It has been estimated that we have done more damage to our soil in the last 70 years than in the whole of human history (Borgström, 1969). The problem is worldwide and can be seen in Haiti, El Salvador, many parts of India, and in Nepal, where, according to that country's national planning commission, 'soil erosion has almost reached the point of no return. It is apparent that the continuation of present trends may lead to the development of a semi-desert type of ecology in the hilly regions' (quoted by Eckholm, 1976). Existing deserts are also spreading. The US government suggests that the Sahara is moving southwards by as much as 30 miles a year at certain points, with human and livestock populations retreating before it, so increasing the pressures on the fringe areas and leading to further desertification. It is estimated that over the past 50 years, 650 000 km^2 of arable land have been absorbed by the spreading Sahara (Eckholm, 1976). In the UK we are fortunate in having excellent soils, but nonetheless, in its evidence to the Strutt Committee (Agricultural Advisory Council, 1970) the National Farmers' Union emphasised the existence of soil deterioration. 'There is no doubt,' it said, 'that real problems exist in some parts of the country, and that these are considered as arising from the systems of cropping and cultivation which have been practised.' The US National Academy of Sciences has estimated that the US has lost already about one third of its topsoil. It may take about 300 years to reproduce 25 mm of topsoil in undisturbed conditions.

Soil erosion is not the only way in which the world is losing its agricultural land. As a result of the population explosion, agricultural land is being lost constantly to housing and industrial estates, motorways, etc. Usually, urban development takes place in the valleys and on the plains, where land is most fertile, so the loss is all the more serious. England and Wales seem to be losing agricultural land at something approaching 15 000 ha/annum (Best, 1976). In Canada, it has been estimated that 1·2 Mha of good agricultural land have been lost in this way between 1961 and 1971 (Geno, 1975). In the USA it is estimated that 400 000 ha of land are lost to urbanisation each year (Frink, et al., 1975).

Higher capital investment is also a problem. It takes about 1500 t of water to grow a tonne of wheat, about 4000 t to grow a tonne of rice, and 10 000 t to grow a tonne of cotton fibre (Revelle, 1963). The cost of bringing new, often marginal, land into cultivation and of renovating existing irrigation systems and building new ones amount to very large figures indeed which, to amortise, will mean a substantially higher price for food.

I have no doubt that there will be major achievements and tragic setbacks during the process of increasing world food supply. The problem is daunting, particularly because the increase in food production is arithmetical, whereas the increase in population is geometrical. Each increment in food output does nothing to facilitate the next increment. Of course, this is not the case with population growth. I know this has been said before, but that does not detract from its validity. You are all familiar with the story of the man who jumps from the fortieth floor of a skyscraper against the advice of his friends. Thirty five floors further down he looked up with a self satisfied smile and said: 'So far, so good!'

It is within this general context that I would like to consider the question of the quality of our food. Unfortunately, under great pressure, we all tend to adopt expedients. When there is great pressure on supply or costs, then quality is sacrificed. We see this in agriculture, when rotation of crops is abandoned, when we create vast stretches of monoculture, and, generally, when we take out more than we put in so as to produce more in the short term. This is equally true in the food industry generally and in intensive farming. The intensive farmers remind us that, if we want a growing population, abundant food and reasonably priced food, then we need to adopt practices which allow for fast, efficient, economic and mass breeding and rearing of animals. Perhaps this is true. But unfortunately, whether we like it or not, and whether we admit it to ourselves or not, these practices result in sacrificing quality for quantity. By quality I do not mean just culinary taste. I mean nutritional value, and the long term effect on our health and on that of our children. Intensively reared animals are different. They live in totally artificial conditions. They are fed differently and they receive, directly or indirectly, unnatural quantities of hormones, antibiotics and other chemicals to speed their growth and to protect them from infectious diseases. I do not propose to discuss the moral case for or against rearing animals in this concentrated way. I would rather touch on some of the physical differences that seem to be the result of intensive production. Some intensively reared poultry are injected after slaughter with substances which result in the retention of water. Thus, part of the increase in the size and weight of the bird is directly attributable to the fact that it has retained water unnaturally. Also, research carried out at the Nuffield Institute of Comparative Medicine has found that the fat content of intensively reared and free-range livestock is different. Animals lay down two kinds of fat: adipose storage fat, consisting mainly of non-essential saturated fats, and structural fats, rich in essential long chain polyunsaturated fatty acids. In free-ranging animals there appears to be roughly one part of adipose fat to three parts of structural fat. In intensively reared animals these figures seem to be reversed. It is adipose fat that is associated with some diseases of degeneration caused by the overconsumption of animal fats. Structural fats contain high proportions of phospholipids, which are essential in the production of nerve tissue. Since nerve cells, including those in the brain, develop during early childhood, and since the structure, once complete, cannot be regenerated, some have claimed that any interference with the intake of phospholipids in young children may have serious and irreversible effects. Furthermore, the long term effects of the use of hormones have still not been assessed satisfactorily. The industry could be marketing products with unknown long term hazards.

The reports of health inspectors who carry out autopsies on intensively bred animals make grisly reading. A high proportion of animals have some form of disease at the time of slaughter (Association of Public Health Inspectors, 1973). Current regulations in the UK do not forbid the sale for human consumption of carcases from which diseased portions have been removed. As a result of these unnatural practices we are creating products that differ more and more from their natural counterparts. So we treat them with artificial colouring agents and with artificial flavouring agents, to try to make them resemble the real thing. And we do not even really know the long term effects of the use of many of these colouring and flavouring agents.

All this is well known and well documented and, as usual, we all try to blame the other fellow. The industry, the government, the health inspectors, the intensive farmers, successively all will become the whipping boys. The truth, of course, is that individually and collectively, we are all responsible. And I hasten to add that I accept fully my share of the blame as a member of the industry and as a member of the public. Collectively we buy, eat, serve, advertise, produce and sell these products, and like practically every other aspect of our national life we refuse to consider the long term effects of our actions and our only interest is in the immediate, short term profits. I would like to make a few somewhat more specific points.

(1) For so long as the world fails to control the growth of population, there will be growing pressure on food supplies and more expedients will be used. These expedients will lead to consequences which will be counter-productive, which in turn will lead to diminishing returns, to further pressure on supplies, and to further expedients which will affect our health and our economy. As these pressures grow, so will the vulnerability of our supplies. There will be good harvests and there will be bad harvests. The former will lull us into a false sense of security, and the latter will lead to famine, on a scale far greater than we have currently, and will affect countries whose peoples still believe that the supply of food is their automatic right. As pressures build, so will the need for more capital investment, and therefore so will the price of food increase. Then, food will be sold principally to those countries which can afford to pay for it.

(2) In Britain, we have had a number of policies for the supply of our food. Until 1846, agriculture was a major and protected industry. This was due partly to the fact that the great rural landlords were the people who controlled the country. In 1846, with the repeal of the Corn Laws, came a great change. It signalled the passing of power from the landlords to the urban barons, and also the decision that food should be procured inter-nationally as cheaply as possible, even at the cost of British agriculture, so as to feed the vast new urban population that was the product of the industrial revolution. In 1846, this was a reasonable policy to pursue. World population at that time was about 1171 million (Population Council, 1974). Britain wanted to become a great industrial nation and this meant that it needed to attract to industrial centres the population that then was

employed on the land. At the same time, we had a great empire, and we could buy agricultural produce from that empire and thereby transmit some wealth to those countries with which they in turn could buy the consumer products manufactured by our industry. It was a policy that clearly was in line with Britain's general economic thinking and imperial position. Except during the blockades of the two world wars, the cheap food policy worked well for us. It is interesting to note that the full effects of the repeal of the Corn Laws on British agriculture were not felt until about 1890. By that time, North America had been opened up and cereal farmers in the prairies had access by rail to eastern sea ports. Immigrant British farmers in Australia and New Zealand were beginning to export food to the home country, and Reece's freezing machine, invented in 1867, was making it possible to transport meat over long distances. The effect is well demonstrated by the price of wheat. In 1812, wheat in Britain was selling for £29 6s/cwt. By 1894 the price had dropped to 5s 4d. The 1812 price was not reached again until 1952, 140 years later (Ministry of Agriculture, Fisheries and Food, 1968). As a result, farming in Britain became deeply depressed, and we became dependent on world surpluses for our food—more so than any other major country. We produce now only about half our requirements of food and we import the other half, but, when imports of foodstuffs and fertilisers are taken into account our true level of dependence on overseas suppliers is even greater: 43% of our wheat, 70% of our sugar, 78% of our butter, 100% of our maize grain, 41% of our meat, 72% of our feedingstuffs, as well as almost all our fertilisers (Allaby, et al., 1975).

The third phase of Britain's strategic planning for food is now overdue. Obviously, conditions have changed totally since the last decisive action of 1846. Overall world surpluses have disappeared, except for the occasional 'mountains', on which great play is made and which still continue to bluff the innocent and the misinformed. So a policy based on feeding our people by buying at bargain prices other people's surpluses, surpluses which are, at best, uncertain, is not a very worthwhile strategy. This is quite apart from the fundamental change that has taken place in our industrial and imperial position in the world. But we are fortunate in that our population is stabilising, our land is fertile and we are part of the Common Market which can, with proper planning, become largely self sufficient in food. I believe, therefore, that our strategy should be to ensure that we supply a substantial proportion of our own food, and that we do so in a balanced way so that we have independence in each of the vital areas of food, and that we should do so within the context of the Common Market agricultural policy.

This would also have a considerable impact on our balance of payments. Our food import bill amounts to nearly £4000 m/annum.

(3) The government has produced recently a white paper under the

title *Food from Our Own Resources* (Ministry of Agriculture, Fisheries and
Food, 1975). This document shows that serious thought is being given to
the subject. But it is not comprehensive enough, it does not go far enough,
and in some ways it goes in the wrong direction. It more or less neglects
the whole area of nutritional quality and, so far as production is concerned, it suggests increases in the production of beef, pigmeat, poultry-
meat and eggs which together exceed the suggested increase in production
of cereals that are to feed them. Thus, we are to increase our imports in
order to produce more of the higher priced items. This trend would carry
us in the direction of Dutch agriculture, where production of livestock
exceeds by a large margin the production of the grain necessary to feed
that livestock. One could consider that farming in the Netherlands has
become part of the food processing industry. It has become a conversion
industry, where livestock converts imported vegetable proteins into
animal protein. The danger inherent in this position can be demonstrated
by what has happened to soya over the past few years. The soya bean will
not grow commercially in northern Europe. The main alternative livestock
protein, Peruvian anchovies, practically disappeared during 1973. As a
result, European livestock herds and flocks became largely dependent on
soya imported from the USA. However, as soon as the first signs of a
shortage of soya became apparent, the USA banned temporarily its export.
We must always remember that countries export only food which is
surplus to their own requirements. No democratic country can be expected
to export food needed for its own population.

If we wish to produce a substantial proportion of our own food needs,
and to do so in a balanced way which guarantees us some independence,
then we must accept that this means long term planning and stability for
the farmer. The farmer cannot be asked to compete with short term surpluses which would disrupt totally his economic planning. This, of course,
is the main fallacy in the talk about particular food 'mountains'. Every
now and then there will be a surplus of one particular commodity in
Europe. This will result from unusually good weather or from a hiccup in
planning. If, when we see this mountain, we say: 'What a good thing. We
can sell this product really cheaply to the housewife,' the result will be the
destruction of the possibility of our farmers producing that commodity
economically, because their price will have been shattered artificially.
We must learn to forgo the occasional bargain so as to provide the
necessary stability to our farmers and thereby ensure our own independence,

(4) I do not believe that our long term plans can be based exclusively
on short term considerations. The nation must be able to feed itself, defend
itself, and fuel its industry. This last consideration is being planned for by
the development of our coal resources and of North Sea oil. It is expected
that the average landed cost of North Sea oil will be well above that of oil
imported from Saudi Arabia. Rightly, this does not deter us from develop-

ing our oil resources in the North Sea. But the potential of our agriculture is as great, is longer lasting, and will be every bit as economic.

(5) We must attempt constantly to maintain a prudent balance between quality, quantity and cost. Of course, to feed a population as large as our own from a land mass of only 240 000 km^2, we must benefit from technology, from industry and from capital. But we must do so without ever forgetting that we must not destroy the long term for short term advantage. We must put back into the land what we take out, and we must be willing to reduce apparent productivity so as to produce products which are good for the long term health of our children. This seems so obvious that it should not need saying, and yet, in my view, we are now doing the opposite.

(6) The structure of government should be altered to reflect the need for overall planning. There should be a Minister of Food. He would be the overlord with general responsibility. Reporting to him should be five Ministers with particular responsibilities. They would be the Minister of Agriculture and Fisheries, the Minister for the Manufacture and Distribution of Food, the Minister of Nutrition, the Minister for the Common Market Agricultural Policy and, finally, a Minister concerned with the Price of Food. Only in this way can we have balanced, overall planning. It is evident that each of these responsibilities are interdependent, and that the Minister of Food should be the overall arbiter.

I know that our leaders have more pressing problems, but I believe that they have few of more fundamental importance.

REFERENCES

Agricultural Advisory Council (1970). *Modern Farming and the Soil*, HMSO, London.

Allaby, M., Blythe, C., Hines, C. and Wardle, C. (1975). *Losing Ground*, Earth Resources Research Ltd, London.

Association of Public Health Inspectors (1973). *Environmental Health Report*, London.

Best, R. H. (1976). 'The extent and growth of urban land', *The Planner*, January, 8, London.

Borgström, G. (1969). *Too Many, A Study of the Earth's Biological Limitations*, Macmillan, London.

Brown, L. R. (1974). *In The Human Interest*, W. W. Norton and Co. Inc. for the Aspen Institute for Humanistic Studies, New York.

Eckholm, E. (1976). *Losing Ground*. In preparation.

FAO (1974). *Assessment of the World Food Situation*, Background paper prepared for the World Food Conference, Rome.

FAO (1975). *Yearbook of Fishery Statistics*, Rome.

Frink, C. R., Horsfall, J. G. and Brown, L. R. (1975). Statements made at the 'Limits to Growth' conference held in October 1975 at Woodlands, Texas.

Geno, L. (1975). 'Energy, Agriculture and the Environment', Study commissioned by Environment Canada. Unpublished.

Holmes, W. (1971). 'Efficiency of food production by the animal industries'. In *Potential Crop Production*, edited by P. F. Wareing and J. P. Cooper, Heinemann Educational Books, London.

Lockeretz, W., Klepper, R., Commoner, B., Gertler, M., Fast, S., O'Leary, D. and Blobaum, R. (1975). *A Comparison of the Production, Economic Returns, and Energy Intensiveness of Corn Belt Farms that do and do not use Inorganic Fertilizers and Pesticides*, Center for the Biology of Natural Systems report CBNS-AE-4, St. Louis, Miss.

Ministry of Agriculture, Fisheries and Food (1968). *A Century of Agricultural Statistics: Great Britain* 1866–1966, HMSO, London.

Ministry of Agriculture, Fisheries and Food (1974). *EEC Agricultural and Food Statistics*, HMSO, London.

Ministry of Agriculture, Fisheries and Food (1975). *Food from Our Own Resources*, Cmnd 6020, HMSO, London.

Ministry of Agriculture, Fisheries and Food (1976). *Annual Review of Agriculture*, HMSO, London.

National Academy of Sciences (1972). *Genetic Vulnerability of Major Crops*, Washington, D.C.

Owen, M. (1973). 'Resources under pressure—water'. In *Intensive Agriculture and the Environment*. CICRA (International Centre for Co-operation in Agricultural Research) Symposium, An Foras Talúntais, Dublin.

Population Council (1974). *Reports on Population, Family Planning*, No. 15, New York.

Revelle, R. (1963). 'Water'. In *Plant Agriculture*, p. 96, readings from *Scientific American*, W. H. Freeman, San Francisco.

US Department of Agriculture (1974). *Stabilization and Price Support Programs 1974*, USDA, Washington, D.C.

PART 1

FOOD REQUIREMENTS OF PEOPLE

CHAPTER 2

Demographic determinants: the World and Britain

W. BRASS

London School of Hygiene and Tropical Medicine

The broad picture of current and prospective growth of world population has been given frequent exposure but it is useful to begin with the following summarised account of the orthodox demographic view of a few years back.

Separate treatment is needed for the developed and less developed, that is the rich and the poor countries, since the outlook for the two groups is very different but the features for the populations in any one group are largely similar. Some 70% of the world's population is in the poor countries (most of Asia, Africa and Latin America) and 30% in the rich (Europe, North America, Australia, Japan and some areas of Latin America). In the rich countries on average 1000 women give birth to 1300 daughters over their reproductive period. Less than 50 of the daughters die before the cohort reaches the maternal ages in turn, and therefore the women are being replaced by 25% more females in the next generation, a growth rate of around 1% per year. The indications are that parents' desire for children is still strong and that population growth will continue at about the same level.

In the poor countries on average 1000 women give birth to 2800 daughters but about 30% of these die before reaching maternal ages. Thus some 2000 replace the initial thousand women giving a doubling of the population in a generation or a growth rate of about 2·6% per year. Mortality in these countries is still very much higher than in the rich areas but is falling fast. The 30% of daughters dead before the maternal ages is likely to decrease towards the 4% or so of the rich countries exerting an upwards pressure on growth rates. However, there are marginal signs of falls in fertility in a few small areas of the less developed world. As the standard of living increases it is to be expected that this trend will become more pronounced but change is likely to be slow. It is hard to strike a balance but it may be near a roughly constant growth rate over the next 25 years or so with some slowing thereafter.

For the world as a whole the net outcome of these considerations is an expected population increase over the period up to the year 2000 of 2%

per year, with the rich and poor groups expanding at their own relatively constant rates. The differential in rates would, however, lead by the end of the 20th century to the proportion of the population in the rich countries falling to 22% as compared with the initial 30%.

The United Nations world population projections (1966, 1973, 1974) fill in these broad outlines in detail for individual countries, with estimates of prospective fertility and mortality levels and trends varying in each. The wide perspective required by the uncertainty about the future, however, imposes a uniformity which ensures that the aggregation does not produce new features about the world scene. The medium projection as calculated in 1968 arrived at populations in the year 2000 for the rich and poor groups of 1454 and 5040 millions, little different from the numbers estimated in 1963. The corresponding aggregates from the 1973 revision give 1368 and 5039 millions for a total of 6407. There has been a slight decrease in the population arrived at for the developed countries but for practical purposes the world growth from 1970 to the end of the century is the same at around 77%.

Even in 1973 there were indications that a fundamental re-appraisal of the assessment of population prospects was due. By 1976 the signs have become too obvious to ignore. As yet, however, the evidence provides an inadequate basis upon which to build a coherent structure. All forecasts must be uncertain but the provision of future estimates implies a degree of belief in the regularity of trends which is difficult to attain in periods of rapid change. In the present situation the rapid change is partly in the current rates and partly in ideas about determinants of population growth. Over the past few years there has been a huge expansion of research into the relation between demographic movements and socio-economic influences. Much of this work has been of poor quality and most of the findings either unconvincing or difficult to interpret. The interactions and the failure to confirm the constraints on change which had been expected have, however, contributed to doubts about the orthodox viewpoint on the prospects of population growth. The range of possibilities has become wider. Although it is too early to provide a clear alternative to the familiar picture an outline may be sketched.

There has been a subtle but significant modification of the attitude of population scientists to time scale. Demographic analyses of various kinds but illustrated by the work of Frejka (1973) have demonstrated that the response of population growth to changes in fertility is slow. Thus a drop in fertility initially only affects the numbers of births (unlike mortality which operates at all ages) and thus directly a tiny section of the population. It is not until the reduced numbers of children born themselves become a relatively smaller generation of parents that the full impact of the fertility drop is experienced. Fifty years is, therefore, a more natural unit of time scale for examining the growth implications than years or even decades.

Parallel to this illumination of the constraints has come a greater understanding of how family building practices are an integrated element of a
society and can not be changed substantially without far-reaching alterations in the way of life. Since dramatic reductions in growth rates through
rapid falls in fertility are culturally and technically implausible, the further
horizon becomes of greater significance. The important question now is
not the population size in the year 2000 but in 2050. This can be illustrated
by some calculations of Frejka. On reasonable assumptions about reductions in mortality (alternatives do not modify the general argument) he
estimates that if fertility fell to make the replacement index one over 30
years the population of Africa would be larger than that in 1970 by 80%
in the year 2000 and by 161% in the year 2050. For a reduction to replacement over 70 years the corresponding percentage expansions are 112%
by 2000 and 383% by 2050. The enormous difference in consequence of
the two paths by 2050 compared with the relatively restricted deviation in
2000 is apparent. The United Nations (1974) have recently carried their
projections beyond the year 2000 but with a similar approach and outlook
as for the shorter term exercise. The medium estimates suggest further
growth of more than 70% in world population by 2050 compared with
2000 to just over 11 000 millions.

The acceptance of 2050 as a more rational point of time for the assessment of future population prospects re-emphasises the huge range of
uncertainty which is to some extent disguised by the sluggishness of the
response of growth to changes in fertility. The United Nations projections
implicitly assume a regular transition from high to low fertility in the
poor countries along similar paths to those traversed by the rich countries
in the later 19th and earlier parts of the 20th century. The model is of
falling birth rates closely linked to socio-economic development and
reductions of child mortality. But the intensive research into the demographic transition in different areas of Europe, centred on Princeton
University, has failed to establish any consistent relation of fertility change
with social and economic indicators. Rather it brings out the importance
of less immediate or quantifiable factors such as cultural identity and
transfusion of ideas. [See Coale (1973) for an overview using these results].
It is, thus, far from clear how the Western experience can be applied to the
less developed countries. A case can be argued that once foci of communities with falling fertility have been established in the developing world their
example could be followed quickly by other populations open to the spread
of the same ideas even where socio-economic factors are less favourable.
In England and Wales there was an astonishing time coincidence in the
onset of the fertility decreases around 1875–80 in the different regions
despite a wide range of levels and associated conditions. In 1975, opinion
and attitudes can be communicated widely with greater speed than a
century earlier.

Some support for the hypothesis that foci of fertility change can accelerate both the initiation and development of response can be found in the recent trends in certain countries, although a proper evaluation has yet to be made. Thus the reductions in fertility in such areas as Singapore and Hong Kong are easy to explain in orthodox terms of improvements in levels of living, standards of education, etc., and falls in child mortality. The well established and studied success of the population policy of Taiwan was achieved in rather special political and economic circumstances. But the downturns in fertility in West Malaysia, Sri Lanka, Thailand, apparently Indonesia and possibly South Korea fit less easily into the traditional 'transitional' concepts. Although there is no support for the view that family limitation can be imposed by authority for the good of the community there is much to suggest that the time lag between individual recognition of the need and action to implement it may be greatly shortened. The provision by governments (or with their approval) of the means for family planning limitation on a wide scale can plausibly be implicated as a facilitating factor in most of these cases but there are some exceptions, for example Indians in East Africa (Hill, 1975).

A notable feature in several of these examples has been the rapid rate of the fertility fall, once it has been initiated. The most striking illustration of all is Mauritius where the mean completed family size at current rates was lowered from 5·4 in 1966 to 3·0 in 1973. A combination of circumstances, including the good quality of the census and vital statistics of the island, and the establishment of a family planning evaluation project just at the start of the fertility fall, made it possible for the Mauritius experience to be examined in unique detail (Xenos, 1976). The problems of population pressure had led to a wide acceptance by authoritative groups of the need for fertility reduction. Once initiated the practice of family planning spread from older, high parity mothers to the younger women with only one or two children, from the Chinese to the Indian to the Creole communities at such a pace that within seven years a birth control pattern not very different from that of the developed countries had been established. There are other impressive illustrations both of fertility falls unmatched by anything in the past (*e.g.* Quebec over the past decade or so) and of similar responses by different ethnic communities in the same country. In West Malaysia in the late 1950s the mean completed family size at current rates was about six for the Malays and seven or more for the Chinese and the Indians. By 1972 the measures were five or a little below for all three ethnic groups with little variation. As in Mauritius there were some differences in the extent, timing and pattern of the fall for the different communities but the overwhelming impression is of uniformity rather than diversity.

The consideration of recent demographic trends in a number of less developed countries has suggested that fertility reductions can take place without the socio-economic concomitants of the past and at a greater speed. The extra uncertainty from these findings has been compounded by the fertility behaviour of the potential parents in the rich countries over the past few years. The population of England and Wales can be taken as a convenient reference both because it typifies the patterns of change in the more developed world as a whole and because of our special concern for its progress. Following the demographic distortion caused by the 1939–45 war fertility rose to substantially above the level required for replacement and after a moderate downwards adjustment in the 1950s, recovered to reach a peak in the mid 1960s. At this time the mean completed family size at current rates was about 2·8. Although there was some reduction in the late 1960s the picture at 1970 was still of a post-war period during which fertility was sufficient, if it persisted, for a steady rise in the population size. The official Government projections varied considerably reaching as high as 66 million for the year 2000 as at 1964 but coming down to 58 million for the 1970 based estimates. It was during these years that particular concern about the possible adverse effects of rising population densities on the environment and the quality of life developed. Since 1970 the rate of reduction in fertility has accelerated and in 1975 the mean completed family size at current rates was about 1·8, indicating, when allowance is made for mortality, that replacement of women by daughters in the next generation is only about 85%.

This remarkable drop of approaching 40% in the level of fertility between 1965 and the present has made apparent the precarious basis of the estimates of future population. In fact it has practically destroyed the underlying concepts of regularity upon which the estimates depended. Briefly these were that completed family sizes of generations of woman would remain constant or alter gradually to a new level but that time measures could be more variable as births were postponed or made up. But the present fluctuation is too large to be explained by these ideas. As a consequence recent official population projections have been made by *ad hoc* expedients rather than consistent techniques. It appears likely that we have entered an era of fertility instability as highly efficient birth control makes the response to social and economic conditions, including ideology and intellectual fashions, sharp and widespread. An attempt to provide a new approach for population forecasting in these circumstances has been made (Brass, 1974). A colleague of mine, Basia Zaba, has recently applied this to England and Wales.

Consequent on the current events official population projections have been revised and, for the first time, published as a set of alternative paths of growth, high, central, low and continuing low [Office of Population Censuses and Surveys (1975)]. The increases in population size over 1970 envisaged for the year 2000 range from about 5 million to nearly zero compared with the 10 million estimate made in 1970. The 1975 vital statistics make the attainment of the high variant even more unlikely.

The forecasts made by Basia Zaba give total populations about the level of the central to low variants with increases of 2–4 million (4–8 %) although the time trends of births and age distribution consequences are substantially different from the official estimates.

The United Nations projections for the more developed countries have not yet caught up with the implications of the rapid falls in fertility. But in terms of world population it is necessary to keep these movements in perspective. Relative to the demographic history of England and Wales and its level of fertility the changes have been large. A reduction in mean family size at current rates of about one child is enormous when the mean is around two but less significant in comparison with the less developed countries average of nearly six. A substantial reduction in the 250 million persons by which the more developed countries are expected to grow by the year 2000 will not alter greatly the anticipated world expansion of 2500 million. It is, however, important to remember that the effect on the use of resources would be much more significant. For example it is calculated that the agricultural resources needed to support an average North American are nearly five times those for the average Indian (Brown, 1974).

The preceding discussion has assessed population prospects entirely in terms of fertility change, ignoring the effects of alterations in the mortality component. The United Nations projections assume a steady improvement in mortality at about the rate experienced in recent years. The arguments for paying little attention to the course of deaths in the broad picture of this paper are that its path has been more regular and 'predictable' than for births and that very large deviations would have to be postulated for the assessment to be seriously influenced. Of course, a case can be made that the pressure of increased population sizes on resources, operating mainly through poorer nutrition, could produce significant rises in the incidence of deaths. The quantitative evidence to support the view that such trends are becoming apparent is weak even for countries under the greatest strains and in the developing world as a whole mortality is still falling fast. In an important piece of research Preston (1975) has shown that the relation between the level of mortality and the gross national product per head in a country has been weakening over time. Thus intermediate factors, presumably medical technology and education in the widest sense, are moderating the impact of the level of living on the chances of death. Bangladesh is an illuminating example. Despite the savage misfortunes of the past 15 years there is convincing evidence from recent studies, as yet unpublished, that mortality has continued to decline, if slowly. Although catastrophe can not be ruled out and the health outlook for some countries is gloomy there is no reason as yet to modify the assessment of population prospects because of the mortality component.

What, then, are the alterations of viewpoint which are suggested by recent evidence? In summary, the uncertainty of future estimates of population size and growth has been underlined by the results of historical research, and the recent trends of fertility in the developed and in some less developed countries. There are strong reasons for believing that changes will occur at unprecedented rates once initiated but little guidance on their timing. The most likely forecasts for the developed regions are of growth by the year 2000 considerably less than the 235 million of the latest United Nations projections. For the rest of the world, the sluggishness of the response to fertility change (the 'momentum' effect) makes the probability low that the 2200 million expected increase by the year 2000 will be dramatically in error. It is worth mentioning that there is an associated 'consumption momentum' over and above since projection variants differ largely in the numbers of children with little alteration for adults. If fertility falls are initiated in a substantial part of the less developed regions over the next decade or two, a plausible case can be made that the pace of change will lead to considerably lower population sizes in the year 2050 than have previously been anticipated.

REFERENCES

Brass, W. (1974). 'Perspectives in population prediction: illustrated by the statistics of England and Wales', *J. R. statist. Soc.*, Series A, **137**, 532–583.

Brown, L. R. (1974). *World population and food supplies: looking ahead.* Background paper for the World Population Conference, Bucharest, United Nations Organization, New York.

Coale, A. J. (1973). 'The demographic transition reconsidered'. In *International Population Conference, Liège*, Vol. 1, pp. 53–72, International Union for the Scientific Study of Population, Liège.

Frejka, T. (1973). *The Future of Population Growth: Alternative Paths to Equilibrium*, John Wiley and Sons, New York.

Hill, A. (1975). 'The fertility of the Asian community of East Africa', *Population Studies*, **29**, 355–372.

Office of Population Censuses and Surveys (1975). *Variant Population Projections*, HMSO, London.

Preston, S. (1975). 'The changing relation between mortality level and economic development', *Population Studies*, **29**, 231–248.

United Nations (1966). *World Population Prospects as Assessed in* 1963, United Nations Organization, New York.

United Nations (1973). *World Population Prospects as Assessed in* 1968, United Nations Organization, New York.

United Nations (1974). *World and regional population prospects.* Background paper for the World Population Conference, Bucharest, United Nations Organization, New York.

Xenos, C. (1976). *Fertility Change in Mauritius and the Impact of the Family Planning Programme*, Mimeographed Report (revised).

Zaba, Basia (1975). Unpublished manuscript.

CHAPTER 3

Food is not just for eating

JOHN McKENZIE

London College of Printing

'Every man, woman and child has the inalienable right to be free from hunger and malnutrition in order to develop fully and maintain their physical and mental faculties. Society today already possesses sufficient resources, organisational ability, and technology and hence the competence to achieve this objective. Accordingly the eradication of hunger is a common objective of all the countries of the international community, especially of the developed countries and others in a position to help. It is a fundamental responsibility of governments to work together for higher food production and a more equitable and efficient distribution of food between countries and within countries' (FAO, 1975).

These words were part of the 'Universal Declaration on the Eradication of Hunger and Malnutrition' issued by the World Food Conference in November 1974. They reflected both an earnest desire and increasing concern about the world food problems of the future. But they omitted one fundamental aspect of the fight to eradicate hunger and malnutrition— the fact that each individual by his own freedom of action to a large extent determines his nutritional status.

In their attempts to formalise the distinction between man and all other animals, philosophers spend much time emphasising issues such as 'freedom of will', 'freedom of choice', and 'creator and controller of one's destiny'. In reality such fine distinctions do not only have a basis in man's spirit and soul but in his physiological condition as well. Nowhere is this more apparent than in the study of nutrition. Thus whilst in some physical aspects of life the individual has no direct control over the functions of his body (*e.g.* the beating of his heart) in other respects he has some partial control (*e.g.* breathing). But in the field of food consumption the individual has absolute control at least within the constraints of economic viability— his alone is the decision to eat or not to eat; to eat this food or that; to eat a little or a lot.

This is not of course to suggest that food consumption is totally unrelated to physiological needs. Undoubtedly in part the act of eating is a response, however hidden, to physiological requirements, inherent needs and taste appeal. Thus the individual sitting at his dinner table is in part performing an automatic ritual that resembles in some way the action of, say, breathing.

However, perhaps as a result of some hidden recognition of the crucial nature of the consumption function man, in part at least, also elects to build round food and eating a whole series of issues in no way related to health and nutritional status.

SOCIAL AND ECONOMIC CRITERIA INFLUENCING FOOD CHOICE

Thus food is used as a sociopsychological tool (McKenzie, 1974). It acts as:

an aid to security;
a substitute for maternal creativity;
a means of demonstrating group acceptance, conformity or rebellion, and prestige;
a means of demonstrating mood and personality;
a compensation for denial or an aid to the alleviation of a crisis.

Yet the issues do not even stop here.

The selection of food also reflects economic matters. It requires the planning and successful deployment of the family budget so that individual purchases fit into the overall scheme as far as the money available is concerned, not only in terms of food and drink but in terms of the total pattern of expenditure (McKenzie, 1975).

The culmination of these sociological, psychological or economic issues is an individual decision to single out specific items of food for consumption—very much bringing into play the whole issue of freedom of will, and individuality. But perhaps regrettably with no detailed attention to nutritional needs.

This is not, of course, to suggest that every individual in every purchase considers any or all of these criteria and makes a specific decision. Often another criterion: habit, works in a very different way. The very fact that last year or last week the budget was divided in this way; that the main meal of the week normally comprises these items; that breakfast always includes cereal and the main meal of the day potato, is mostly strong enough to ensure that a similar demand is made the coming week.

In such a context it is perhaps not surprising to find that as a result of all these pressures and, indeed, of the fact that the consumer does not readily acknowledge the need to eat to survive but rather emphasises the pleasure to be gained from food, that individuals seldom achieve maximum efficiency in food choice:

in economic terms we do not seek to satisfy our nutrient requirements as economically as possible (20p a day could provide the food to satisfy nutrient intake if this was the only issue);
in nutrition terms the foods we actually choose may not provide the optimum balance or even the minimum requirements.

It has, of course, long been acknowledged that these issues present fundamental problems in a developing society where the balance between selecting the right foods and surviving and selecting the wrong foods and dying, has always been a narrow one. But in Western society the development of 'the land of plenty' has resulted mostly in the achievement and maintenance of satisfactory nutritional status whatever the individual has chosen to consume. Only three problem groups emerge:

those suffering from overconsumption generally or possibly from the ramifications of too heavy a consumption of particular foods;
those minority groups still vulnerable because of age and poverty;
those with psychosomatic health problems.

Hence one of the fundamental questions for this conference to consider is whether the haphazard nature of our food choice as far as nutrition and economy are concerned is likely to present problems in the future not only in developing countries but also in Western society. Such problems as might emerge in the West could include:

at one extreme the risk of an increasing scarcity of food and therefore the need for us to avoid the waste of scarce resources and to optimise the efficiency of our intake;
at the other extreme the problem of overnutrition related to an ever-increasing abundance of choice and total availability;
in the middle somewhere also the problem of optimum nutrition. Are we moving towards the day when every individual should have a carefully individually prepared diet to which he should adhere strictly so as to correct and compensate for existing deficiencies and to exploit his talents for the maximum maintenance of health and resistance to disease?

My task in this conference is not in a sense to answer these questions but to ensure that we recognise that if these issues reflect possible problems for nutrition for the future then their solution in terms of changing food habits may not be an easy one. Indeed that if change has to be enforced it may not only have manifestations on the individual's physical health but also on his feelings of security and wellbeing and on his personal relationships within society.

Moreover, it means that to ensure that essential change is actually achieved it will be necessary to pursue all possible professional persuasion

methods with great determination—and even then they may be an inadequate tool to overcome the enormous pressures involved.

RECENT CHANGES DUE TO ECONOMIC PRESSURES

This is not of course to suggest that change seldom occurs. The consumer
may resist the change he does not desire but equally he is always adapting
his food habits to match new desires or economic considerations. Nowhere
has this latter aspect been more clear than in the last two years.

The increase in price of all foods during 1974 was approximately 17%
and during 1975 was a further 24% (Table 1). Not surprisingly these price
increases had a colossal impact on food choice. Moreover impact was

TABLE 1

CHANGES IN GROCERS INDEX OF FOOD PRICES 1974–1976 (1 JANUARY, 1968 = 100)

	January 1974	January 1975	December 1975	January 1976	% change Jan 1975/76
All foods	168·04	195·85	237·78	243·05	+24·1
Processed foods	155·20	202·15	228·45	231·46	+14·5
Fresh foods	184·02	187·88	249·32	257·39	+37·0
Beverages	122·32	137·83	147·05	155·75	+13·0
Tea	109·66	114·06	117·60	117·60	+3·1
Coffee	141·14	162·24	180·40	207·34	+27·8
Cereals	167·72	215·94	245·03	246·17	+14·0
Bread	174·42	201·72	238·64	238·64	+18·3
Biscuits	150·57	220·17	235·36	235·36	+6·9
Cakes	152·52	215·32	251·72	254·72	+18·3
Flour	186·76	224·28	218·58	226·52	+1·0
Breakfast cereals	141·73	194·92	218·16	222·01	+13·9
Other	208·11	284·70	306·91	306·91	+7·8
Dairy products	167·15	216·27	244·29	251·52	+16·3
Cheese	175·07	229·05	243·56	255·16	+11·4
Milk, canned and powdered	166·20	208·37	262·96	262·96	+26·2
Cream, canned	131·68	171·42	213·93	213·93	+24·8
Fats	151·21	200·80	211·86	214·26	+6·7
Butter	137·67	161·90	182·77	186·67	+15·3
Margarine	173·52	271·21	273·65	273·65	+0·9
Cooking fats	172·67	255·21	242·96	242·96	−4·8

TABLE 1 (*continued*)

	January 1974	January 1975	December 1975	January 1976	% change Jan 1975/76
Fish	166·74	181·91	210·00	211·74	+16·4
Canned	142·44	147·00	155·53	155·53	+5·8
Frozen	197·49	225·73	278·25	282·16	+25·0
Fruit	127·91	193·66	199·08	199·08	+2·8
Dried	136·07	155·39	155·86	155·86	+0·3
Canned	123·44	214·41	222·56	222·56	+3·8
Meat	175·92	194·04	232·86	236·73	+22·0
Frozen	159·48	184·20	211·08	211·65	+14·9
Canned	154·52	169·51	198·87	199·68	+17·8
Bacon and ham	186·78	205·72	251·42	259·82	+26·3
Sausages, etc.	144·79	191·09	226·82	226·82	+18·7
Sugar and preserves	133·92	311·02	272·45	272·45	−12·4
Sugar	127·21	346·40	283·01	283·01	−18·3
Jam, honey and spreads	147·07	220·05	239·63	239·63	+8·9
Marmalade	157·61	236·82	262·87	262·87	+11·0
Vegetables	134·03	187·36	263·73	240·76	+28·5
Frozen	134·43	150·40	197·62	198·68	+32·1
Canned	149·52	239·47	284·44	284·97	+19·0
Dried and other	115·00	147·28	203·50	213·71	+45·1
Fresh foods					
Meat	210·24	214·01	253·67	257·45	+20·3
Vegetables	163·43	174·90	304·07	372·88	+113·2
Fish	346·59	363·59	423·61	446·85	+22·9
Eggs	170·19	102·57	163·64	128·11	+24·9
Fruit	161·47	231·02	248·43	233·33	+1·0
Milk	124·45	113·14	192·34	192·34	+70·0

greater than might have been expected because of the overall impact of price increases in other fields during the same period. In the short run at least it seems consumers have to cut back on food expenditure before they reduce their expenditure on other items. It is likely that this is because so many of the other items in their budget are fixed, at least in the short run—like HP payments on the car, rent and mortgages—so that the cuts have to come out of the housekeeping. Equally because the severity of the economic situation has hit home so hard, the housewife seems psychologically compelled to take a very critical view of expenditure in the main area for which she is responsible and impose change accordingly.

Thus after a year of this so-called depression (say January 1975), it was possible to identify a number of specific trends in the consumer's behaviour (McKenzie, 1975). First the housewives' attitudes towards shopping seem to have changed. More and more at this time she seemed to be taking time to check out comparative prices in various shops and spread her purchasing activity around to make use of the various bargains available. Equally there was a significant growth in the sales of own label brands from companies such as Tesco, Fine Fare, Sainsburys, Marks & Spencers at the expense of the major manufacturing brand leaders.

Secondly the housewife began to view very much more critically her purchases of convenience products or products that appealed to only certain members of the family. Thus for example there was a big decline in the sale of products such as instant potato (except briefly during the potato shortage), 'complete meals', cakes and expensive personal items such as commercial slimming aids. In Table 2 I identify some of the changes which occurred to other items. It was possible to see a reversal of earlier trends away from 'cheap foods' such as tea and bread, flour, porridge oats, sausages, apples and a particular reduction in 'expensive

TABLE 2

GROWTH TRENDS IN CHEAP AND EXPENSIVE FOODS 1968–1975

(in terms of the percentage change in quantity of specified foods consumed per head per week between the years mentioned)

	1968/73 (%)	1973/74 (%)	1st half 1974/75 (%)
Cheap foods			
Tea	−3	4	0
Bread (white)	−3	3	−5
Flour	0	9	1
Porridge oats	−4	15	−6
Sausages	−1	2	−11
Apples	1	6	−7
Expensive foods			
Frozen vegetables	14	−4	20
Citrus fruit	1	−13	11
Bananas	−2	−3	7
Breakfast cereals	4	−2	5
Buns, scones, tea cakes	−4	−13	20
Slimming, malt and other breads	1	−15	1
Brown bread	−3	−6	33
Baked beans	2	−5	0

foods' such as citrus fruit, buns and tea cakes, slimming, malt and other breads (Mintel, 1975).

Again there was a tendency to reject the purchase of ready prepared items for consumption outside the main meal occasions. Snacks were not seen as important and if somebody had to eat between meals they were much more likely to be asked to make do with the odd left-overs!

All of this led to her increasing return to using basic ingredients to cook the products herself.

But it is interesting to see that some of these trends at least have not continued as the recession period has gone on. Over time it seems that the housewife has been more able to re-adjust the pattern of her expenditure so as to give greater priority to the foods which she really likes. Equally perhaps her psychological guilt at using convenience and expensive items has been reduced. Thus as we moved through 1975 (Table 2) the earlier trends in consumption have re-emerged with the movement away from 'cheap foods' and a movement towards more expensive ones (Mintel Report, 1975). Thus frozen vegetables, buns, scones, tea cakes, brown bread, have shown a further significant jump forward whilst consumption in products such as sausages, white bread and porridge oats has again come to show a decline. This led Mintel to conclude that whilst the future was not clear 'it seems reasonable to suggest that food consumption patterns now look more secure than consumer durables and may be permanently past the worst. The shock of the miners' strike, short time working, etc., was probably more emotionally extreme than that likely from unemployment and the real decline in living standards likely in the future—food is past the worst, leaving durables to bear the continued effect of recession'.

Yet another intriguing situation has been the slowing down on the growth in own-label sales (Mintel, 1976). This in fact reflects two things. First there is a limit to the number of product categories which can justifiably merit an own label product. Thus on the basis of Fine Fare's experience growth rate in terms of the introduction of new products was slowing down very much even by the early 1970s. Secondly, there have been increases in prices, so although the own label product has continued to be say 1p or 2p cheaper with inflation, its significance as a percentage difference between the main brand and own label has declined. Thus in 1975 the percentage difference in price between brand leader and own label products was probably only half what it was in 1973.

THEMES FOR THE FUTURE

So where does all this take us in the next 10 years? Undoubtedly it would be a brave man who would put forward very strong views on this issue now. Indeed the whole issue of a rise or decline in the standard of living in this country as well as the development of technology and the position of world food supplies will have a very significant impact on food trends and nutritional viability. In this sense the questions asked earlier about the absolute nature of where we are going are of relevance. Nevertheless I do believe that it is possible to identify a few trends which are likely to emerge in the 1980s regardless of our standard of living position. I have attempted to identify some of these in the following paragraphs in terms of specific 'themes'. I have also attempted to present each of these in some sort of schematic form (Figs. 1, 2 and 3).

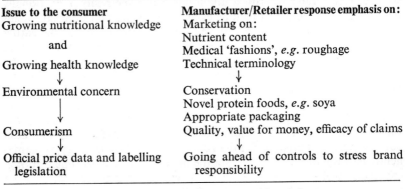

Fig. 1.   *Influence of information and knowledge.*

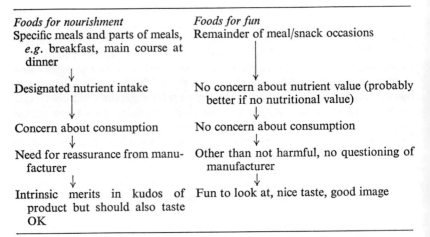

Fig. 2.   *Distinction between foods for nourishment and foods for fun.*

The first theme is undoubtedly 'information and knowledge'. Over the past 10 years or so it has been possible to see a profound growth in the consumer's knowledge of nutrition. This knowledge has probably come primarily from the housewife's concern with slimming. Whether or not one regards this as a desirable motivation it undoubtedly has reinforced her understanding and perception of concepts such as protein, vitamins, carbohydrates, calories and led her to more readily identify the foods that are associated with these properties.

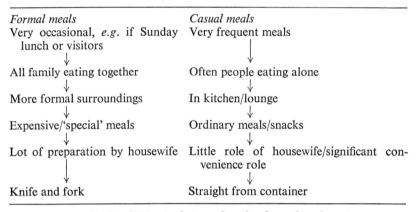

Formal meals	Casual meals
Very occasional, *e.g.* if Sunday lunch or visitors	Very frequent meals
↓	↓
All family eating together	Often people eating alone
↓	↓
More formal surroundings	In kitchen/lounge
↓	↓
Expensive/'special' meals	Ordinary meals/snacks
↓	↓
Lot of preparation by housewife	Little role of housewife/significant convenience role
↓	↓
Knife and fork	Straight from container

Fig. 3.   Distinction between formal and casual meals.

At the same time there has been increasing awareness of health problems in middle and old age that may have a nutritional element such as coronary heart disease.

Again fashionable trends now rapidly move into the consumers vision—thus the roughage story is almost as well known to the housewife as it is to the clinician. By the same token knowledge of world food problems and environmental problems are increasingly understood by the housewife. Hence her recognition of the role of soya and other novel protein products may play in the future.

At a different level consumerism has been growing rapidly with various organisations both on television, wireless and in the press identifying 'best buys', 'buy of the week' and things of this nature. Recently in Chester for the cost of a phone call shoppers could be told the lowest prices at a number of city centre supermarkets and smaller shops with a range of 20 foodstuffs including items such as eggs, meat, bread, fruit and vegetables. At a wider level the government 'Price Check' policy could have considerable impact on consumers' choice of food items.

None of this necessarily means the consumer will, in practice, put optimum nutrition or value for money top of her list of factors influencing food choice. But it does mean she will be mindful of these issues and at least pay lip service to them. I also believe these issues will be reinforced by manufacturers and retailers who will 'jump onto the bandwagon'. I predict they will go far beyond legislative requirements regarding price, nutrient content and the provision of information on their products in an effort to court consumer loyalty.

I would also expect nutrition/health trends to be exploited by the manufacturer in new products. An example of how such themes can be developed may be found in the contemporary situation. Over the last few years it has become apparent that the consumer wants nutritional reassurance and naturalness in a palatable form. At the same time she wants probably more basic foodstuffs which meet the mood of the times.

How has the manufacturer responded? Let us look at the yogurt situation. Basically what existed for many, many years was a product which had many favourable health connotations and which was seen as highly desirable. But it was too expensive and it did not taste right to most people. Then the major manufacturer was able to come onto the scene and build up a product which had elements of the existing product about it but none of its current deficiencies. It was made to taste good, it was made to include fruit and its price was reduced. Moreover it was presented in a marketable form with a reasonable shelf-life in the supermarket. Many of the original devotees of yogurt would argue that the product had now lost everything of essence which it had originally contained in taste terms. But it introduced the product to the public which they found very, very acceptable (Fig. 1).

The second theme which I believe will emerge may be summarised as 'Distinction between foods for nourishment and foods for fun'. In a way this concept stems from the previous one. As consumers become more and more knowledgeable about food, so I think they will clearly distinguish between items of their diet which are of recognisable nutritional significance and which should be 'packed full' of protein, vitamins, etc., and items which are there just as a 'frivolous' addition to the meal and whose whole criteria should be that they taste and look good. Indeed, it may even be desirable that these latter items are 'full of nothingness' with no calories or other nutrients in them so as not to upset any nutritional calculations.

This is not to say that the 'nourishment foods' should be in any sense clinical or savour in any way of medicine. They would be basic 'good' foods. And to a large degree the trend would simply accentuate existing trends. Thus for example breakfast and the main course at dinner time would have the nourishment theme strongly attached to them whilst snacks, desserts, etc., would be there just for fun. Again the manufacturer will probably reinforce such a positioning by implicitly or explicitly categorising his foods in this way (Fig. 2).

The third theme is in a different dimension and, I believe, will be a further manifestation of 'formal meals versus casual meals'. As time passes more and more meals are no longer consumed at a table in the dining room. Indeed in a separate piece of research I have recently undertaken there is a great deal of evidence to show that the sideboard is becoming redundant! Thus many meals are taken either in the kitchen or on the consumer's knee. In the same way items within the meal are taken straight from a package, for example many of the chilled desserts. I suspect that this and the enormous cost of traditional English dishes, such as roast beef and Yorkshire pudding will polarise the situation still further over the next few years. We will be left with a small number of 'formal meals' per week served on traditional occasions, such as Sunday lunch or when visitors come and when expensive, long-established basic foods will be used. It is also likely that they will involve the housewife in using, as best she can, her technical cookery skills. And the end result will certainly be served in a formal setting possibly the separate dining room if such a room still exists. However, most other 'casual meals' will not be served in such a way; they will major on convenience so that the cooking role performed by the housewife as against the manufacturer will be much more limited; they will be confined to simply the family (either as a group or as individuals eating at separate times); often they will be eaten straight out of the container provided by the manufacturer; and very frequently they will be eaten in an armchair (Fig. 3).

REFERENCES

FAO (1975). *Food and Nutrition*, **1**, 41.

McKenzie, J. C. (1974). 'The impact of economic and social status on food choice', *Proc. Nutr. Soc.*, **33**, 67.

McKenzie, J. C. (1975). 'Food prices and the consumer', *Nutrition, Lond.*, **29**, 275.

Mintel (1975). *Signs of the Times*, November, pp. 1–3.

Mintel (1976). *Own Labels*, January, pp. 44–53.

CHAPTER 4

Growing populations and rising aspirations

C. GOPALAN

Indian Council of Medical Research, New Delhi

THE WORLD SCENE

Population growth and its possible effects on the future of mankind, have been the subjects of several futuristic exercises during the last few decades. There have been quite a few grim predictions and gloomy forecasts, some of which have the 'bizarre quality of Old Testament prophecies'. All these exercises in futurism, however, have obvious limitations which are now generally recognised. They are largely in the nature of projections of current trends into the future, and cannot take into account the imponderable factors that may reverse or modify these trends in future. Even so, the forecasts serve the useful purpose of alerting the world as to what *can* happen if present trends continue unchecked. They are thus in the nature of a warning to mankind, to mend its ways, to reorder its life-style and to seek a more harmonious and durable relationship with its environment.

The global sweep of some of these futuristic exercises, implies the assumption that the world is a single economic unit, whose resources are available to all its inhabitants equitably. The threat to human survival posed by expanding populations and diminishing resources would have appeared even more alarming, if the hard realities of the present day world had been taken into account. The process of economic polarisation of the world into the affluent 'haves' and the poor 'have nots' continues on its relentless course. Over half of the world population living in Asia has, today, less than 30% of the world's total food resources, while Europe and North America, which account for less than 30% of the world population, have nearly 60% of the total food supplies. Asia has today nearly 55% of the world's population but enjoys no more than 10% of the world's total income. The recent energy crisis has dramatically highlighted our inability to share and exploit the world's available resources for the maximal benefit of all mankind. What is true of fossil fuels today will become true of a number of other scarce natural resources tomorrow. The statesmen of the world have yet to evolve a new ethos in international

33

relationship which will ensure the judicious exploitation and husband-
ing of the world's available resources for the maximal benefit of all
mankind.

On the other hand, many developing countries of the world have, first,
to put their own houses in order. Today, there are far greater socio-
economic inequalities obtaining in the developing countries of the world
than in the affluent. For example, according to some estimates, nearly 30%
of India's population live below the 'poverty line', meaning that even if
they expend 80% of their income on food, they will not be able to afford
even the least-cost balanced diets recommended by India's National
Institute of Nutrition. And I may here repeat what I have often stated
before. There would be very little malnutrition in India today if all the
food available in the country could be equitably distributed in accordance
with physiological needs. Mere increase in food production will not solve
the problem of malnutrition unless the purchasing power of the poor
segments is raised to levels at which they can buy the foods they require
and, in respect of much child malnutrition, unless mothers apprehend the
nutritional needs of their children and learn to feed them appropriately.
Malnutrition is thus not a function of food production alone but also very
much of food distribution as well. The important determinant of malnutrition in many developing countries is not just the size of the population
but the proportion of that population which is unemployed or under-
employed. Institutional changes and reforms aimed at reducing socio-
economic disparities can thus make as significant a contribution to
improved nutrition in many developing countries as control of population
growth or increase of food production. In any consideration of the
problems of population and food, we will have to clearly recognise these
hard realities.

We can distinguish two contrasting trends as between the affluent
countries and the developing countries, both with regard to the pattern of
population growth as well as the pattern of food production and
consumption.

Population growth

Let us first consider the pattern of population growth. Many developing
countries have populations expanding at the rate of 2·5–3·5% per year. In
Europe, on the other hand, the rate is around 0·5% and is practically at
zero in a number of countries. Infant and child mortality in most affluent
countries is already so low that there is not much scope for further
improvement. On the other hand in many developing countries, death
rates which are still high may be expected to show a continuing decline
over the next few decades. While life expectancy has been showing a
steady and substantial increase in many developing countries, in the
affluent countries life expectancy has remained either stationary or indeed

in some cases has actually shown a decline. Medical science has still no satisfactory answers to the problems of heart disease and cancer, the major killers in affluent societies.

As a result of these contrasting trends in fertility and mortality, a preponderant proportion of increase of world population in the next two decades will be accounted for by increase in the populations of developing countries. It has been computed that the world population, which stood at around 3600 million in 1970, may exceed 6600 million by 2000 A.D., and nearly 90% of this increase will be accounted for by increase in the populations of Africa, Asia and Latin America. For example, at the present growth rate, India's population will approach 1000 million by the turn of the century. The present annual increase in India's population is of the order of 15 million—about the total population of Australia or Holland. The picture with regard to population growth in the rest of Asia is no less alarming. Such population increase may be expected to greatly accentuate pressure on the already severely strained facilities for health care, food, housing and education in these countries.

Food production
Let me now turn to the patttern of food production and food consumption; and I shall deal with food production first. In the affluent countries, the prevailing trend is for larger and larger farms to be managed by fewer cultivators. On the other hand, in many of the poor countries, smaller and smaller farms have to be cultivated by the same or an even larger number of farmers. The highly mechanised, capital-intensive and labour-saving technology of the affluent countries is not only not feasible but entirely inappropriate in the developing countries, given the prevailing conditions. Also, agricultural operations in affluent countries are based on high consumption of energy derived from non-renewable resources of the earth. Thus, Dr Swaminathan (1973) points out that, while in 1964, about 280 kcal (1·2 MJ) of energy were needed in countries like India and Indonesia to produce 1 kg of rice protein, in the United States as much as 2860 kcal (12 MJ) of energy were needed to produce 1 kg of wheat protein, and over 65 000 kcal (272 MJ) to produce 1 kg of beef protein. While 96% of the energy input in the United States in 1970 came from oil, gas and coal, in the same year non-commercial fuels like cow dung, firewood and wastes provided nearly 60% of India's energy needs. If the rest of the world should copy the American technology for food production, the world's oil wells will run dry within two decades. The greatest challenge that faces the poor countries of the world is the 'development of technologies where the productivity of land can be continuously increased with diminishing dependence on non-renewable sources of energy by deploying recycling processes more and more effectively'. This is a challenge that will eventually face affluent countries.

Food consumption

Now for the pattern of food consumption. Two contrasting food chains are in evidence as between the affluent countries on the one hand and the poor developing countries on the other. The latter depend largely on the plant–man food chain, unlike the former which depend on the plant–animal–man food chain. Out of the average annual *per caput* consumption of food grains of about 1 tonne in the affluent nations, only about 70 kg are consumed directly, while the remaining 930 kg are used as animal feed to raise meat, milk and eggs for human consumption. In contrast, the annual *per caput* consumption of grain in the developing countries is about 190 kg, most of which is directly consumed. Thus, the implications of food grain shortage are totally different as between a country like India and a country like the USSR. In one case, food grain shortage may mean starvation, while in the other it may mean a reduction in the current high levels of intake of animal protein. The daily intake of protein in the diet of adults of developing countries is of the order of 50 g, a level which is adequate to meet the protein needs, and the protein is largely derived from vegetable sources. As against this, the daily intake of protein in the diet of adults of many affluent countries exceeds 100 g daily and the protein is largely derived from animal sources, an intake which is clearly far in excess of physiological needs. Perhaps the demand for meat is a reflection of rising aspirations, but this surely is an aspiration that should be consciously suppressed.

It will thus be obvious that in the context of growing populations and diminishing resources, human survival in an interdependent world, demands concerted action by both rich and poor nations on four major lines, namely:

> drastic curbs on population growth;
> correction of socio-economic disparities in order to facilitate a more equitable distribution of available food;
> curbs on excessive use of non-renewable resources of the earth and development of alternative, appropriate technologies that will ensure increased food production with minimal reliance on such resources;
> curbs on wasteful overconsumption of food grains through excessive diversion of food grains for animal feeding.

THE INDIAN SITUATION

The major question of interest to this conference is whether world food production can keep pace with population growth. Since India accounts for nearly one seventh of the world's population, the Indian experience may provide some indications in this regard.

Population growth

The population of India, which was around 250 million at the beginning of the century, rose to 350 million in 1950, an increase of nearly 100 million in 50 years. During the next 25 years the population rose to nearly 600 million, an increase of about 250 million. Even according to optimistic estimates which allow for vigorous implementation of the family planning programme, India's population will reach 950 million by the turn of the century. It may be pointed out that since 1960, the government of India had accorded high priority to family planning programmes. Measures to control fertility have been recently further intensified. Even so, an increase of population of the order mentioned above seems probable.

In India, as indeed in all developing countries, the major factor responsible for the rapid growth of population has been the sharp decline in mortality rates. Thus India's mortality rate declined from nearly 45/1000 at the beginning of the century to 16/1000 in 1971 and is expected to further decline to less than 8/1000 by 2000 A.D. Life expectancy has shown a steady increase. In the face of such spectacular decline in mortality, even the most vigorous fertility control programmes have failed to bring about the desired reduction in the growth rate. It may be several years before the full impact of India's family planning programmes becomes manifest. India's population is expected to get stabilised at a stationary level only several years after 2000 A.D., by which time it would have more than doubled its present size.

The problem of population growth has not only a quantitative but a qualitative dimension as well. The increase in India's population during the next few decades will be associated with a change in the age structure (Fig. 1). Thus, while children under 14 years of age constituted more than

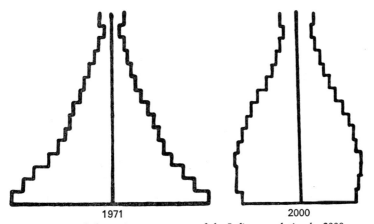

1971   2000

Fig. 1.   Expected change in age structure of the Indian population by 2000 A.D.
(expressed in 5 year intervals).

40% of the total population in 1971, they will constitute less than 30% of the total population in 2000 A.D. While from the point of view of productivity this reduction in the 'dependency load' may be considered favourable, this will also imply that the increase in actual food requirement will be greater than what may be inferred from increase in population size (Table 1). Increase of population in the next few decades will also be

TABLE 1

DEPENDENCY LOAD OF CHILDREN AND OLD PERSONS (1971–2001)

Dependents (i.e. *aged* 0–14 *and* 60 +)/100 *persons in* 15–59 *age group*

	0–14	60 +	Total
1971	78·0	9·6	87·7
1981	70·7	9·9	80·6
1991	59·5	10·8	70·3
2001	46·0	12·1	58·1

associated with increasing urbanisation. According to one UN report (1973), the proportion of urban population to total population in Asia and the Far East will increase from the present 25% to 43% by 2000 A.D. This may also be expected to affect the pattern of food consumption.

Food production

We may now turn to the question 'Can India's food production in the coming decades be adequately increased to meet the demands of its growing population?' The population of India rose from 360 million in 1950 to 440 million in 1960. The food grain production during the same period rose from 55 Mt to 85 Mt. This increase was brought about by bringing more land under cultivation. Between 1961 and 1975, the population of India rose from 440 million to 600 million. During the same period, food grain production registered an increase from 85 Mt to 118 Mt. This increase was achieved through increased yield per hectare, brought about by high-yielding varieties of food grains and improved agricultural technology. Thus during the two decades (1951–1971), a period characterised by extraordinarily rapid population growth, the *per caput* availability of food grains actually increased from 303 g/day in 1951 to 460 g/day in 1971. Contrary to the general belief, the levels of food imports were relatively insignificant, being usually around 2% and nearing 10% in just one year, levels which were certainly no greater than those of USSR or China (Table 2). Thus, so far, in general, increase in food grain production in India has more than managed to outstrip population growth. But what of the future?

A careful examination of India's performance in the agricultural field over the last two decades would show that, despite some spectacular gains, the country was unable to exploit her resources and technological potential to the full. It was no doubt true that there was an impressive increase in food grain production, but this was an increase largely confined to cereals.

TABLE 2

POPULATION AND FOOD PRODUCTION

Year	Population (millions)	Food grain production (Mt)	Per caput availability g/day
1951	360	55	303
1975	600	118	460

The production of pulses, important sources of protein in the Indian diet, actually declined. Even among cereals, the increase was largely attributable to wheat and to a less extent to rice. While wheat production rose from 11 Mt in 1965 to 27 Mt in 1971, millets which constitute the major staple of the diet of poor segments of the population did not register a significant increase. Also there was considerable instability in the performance from year to year. Inputs in fertilisers and extension of irrigation fell far short of requirement. The total fertiliser input was around one million tons annually and only less than 17% of cultivable land received assured irrigation. Average yields per hectare over the country were far less than in USA, Japan or Egypt. Indian agriculture is still very much at the mercy of the monsoon, and in the absence of assured irrigation modern methods of intensive agricultural technology are not feasible over large areas. Post-harvest losses of food grains during storage are quite considerable. India's immense water resources have yet to be fully harnessed, as evidenced by frequent episodes of alternating floods and droughts in different parts of the country. The vast marine food resources available in India's long coastline have also remained largely untapped.

The fact that India has not, as yet, fully exploited her resources and potential, offers at once a challenge, and the hope that if the current constraints are overcome and the mistakes of the past avoided, India can in fact boost her food production to levels commensurate to the needs of her growing population.

Future food requirements
There are several possible approaches towards estimating future food requirements. The National Institute of Nutrition constructed a low-cost

balanced diet based on generally accepted figures for nutrient requirements and taking into account the dietary habits of the population. On this basis and expected population growth, the Institute estimated India's future food requirement. According to this exercise, the order of food grain production that would be needed by 2000 A.D. would be around 180 Mt; milk production has to be increased by 100%, production of edible oil, meat and eggs by 300% over the 1970 levels in order to meet the requirement in 2000 A.D. The National Commission on Agriculture, whose report has just been released, has computed the future food demands on the basis of expected population growth and expected changes in income, and has estimated the demands for food grains in 2000 A.D. as between 170 and 180 Mt and that the demands for milk, fish, meat and oil will represent an increase of nearly 200%, and that for eggs nearly 400% over the 1970 figures. The Commission estimates allow for an increase of *per caput* energy intakes from the present 2080 kcal/day (8·7 MJ/day) to 2500 kcal/day (10·5 MJ/day) in 2000 A.D.

The Commission then proceeds to examine the possibilities of meeting these demands. An increase of food grain production to around 180 Mt in 2000 A.D. should be perfectly feasible if irrigation can be extended to 40% (Table 3) of the cultivable land as against the present 17% and if

TABLE 3

INDIA'S FOOD NEEDS IN 2000 A.D. (MT)

	1971	2000
Food grains	100	180
Milk	23	65
Meat	0·7	2
Fish	2	7
Eggs (number)	6 000 m	28 000 m

fertiliser input can be stepped up from the present level of under 2 Mt to at least 14 Mt by 2000 A.D. Increase of milk production from the current level of 23 Mt to 65 Mt in 2000 A.D. would be possible if the current programmes for the improvement of the productivity of cattle and buffaloes, through cross breeding with superior breeds; better feeds; adequate health cover and proper marketing facilities, can be implemented. Raising egg production from the current output of 6000 million to 28 000 million by 2000 A.D., and augmenting the meat production from the current output of 680 000 t annually to 2 Mt in 2000 A.D., are also technologically feasible. India has a coastline of 5600 km and vast resources for inland fisheries. This potential is as yet largely untapped as also the considerable molluscan resources. In the opinion of the Commission the prospects of raising fish production from the current level of under 2 Mt to nearly 7 Mt in 2000 A.D. are quite reasonable. The Commission concludes on the optimistic note that it will be possible for India to achieve the quantities and the range of food production needed by the population in 2000 A.D. and has set out the strategy to be followed for this purpose.

Forecasting the future food situation in relation to population growth is admittedly a hazardous exercise. But, it can at least be said that on the basis of all the information currently available, India has the resources and the technological potential to feed a population of the size expected in 2000 A.D. Whether in fact this potential will be realised in practice will be determined by the manner in which India's agricultural and food programmes are managed and implemented.

EFFECTS OF POPULATION PRESSURE ON THE FOOD SUPPLY

Most predictions and forecasts on the impact of population growth on the nutritional situation have followed the conventional Malthusian logic. When we look back on the Indian experience, however, we find that some of the worst famines in Indian history occurred when the total population of the country was less than a third of the current level. There is an official record of severe famine in North India in 1630–1632 at the time of the Emperor Shah Jehan, the builder of the famous Taj Mahal. At the time of Robert Clive in Bengal, in the early days of the British Empire in India, history records that half of Bengal was wiped out by famine. Again in the latter half of the 19th century, Madras was the site of a disastrous famine, and the book on *Diseases of the Madras Famine* written by Alexander Porter (1889) out of his experiences then, remains unparalleled as the most informative medical chronicle on famine anywhere. Also in the Bengal famine which occurred towards the close of British rule in India, the total number of deaths from starvation exceeded the total casualties of the Allies during the entire course of the Second World War. Indeed during all this long period in Indian history, India's population remained more or less stationary.

During the last 25 years, India's population has increased enormously. And yet, while it is true that the nutritional status of large segments of the poor population is by no means satisfactory, large-scale famines of the type seen in earlier years have not occurred. In fact even the much publicised Bihar famine was 'a famine that never was'. Cases of famine oedema which used to be frequently seen in Madras, even in times of no famine some 30 years ago, are rarely seen today. Cases of acute cardiac beriberi which used to be a common occurrence in some parts of the country 25 years ago are no longer seen. This is not to deny that there is still considerable malnutrition among the poor vulnerable segments of the population, but there is no evidence that its severity or frequency has increased. It may be concluded that contrary to general expectation, the sharp increase in India's population during the last 25 years has not aggravated the problem of malnutrition in the country.

I had started my presentation with the statement that some of the predictions and forecasts we have heard are akin to Old Testament prophesies. Paul and William Paddock, for example, predicted that widespread famine and hunger would overtake India in the year 1975 on the basis of some theoretical calculations. By a strange coincidence the year 1975 proved to be the year when India recorded its highest production of food grain. There are other predictions which have set the date of disaster for India at 1985. All this raises the question of the very soundness of Malthusian logic and highlights the potential fallacies in forecasting the food situation in relation to population growth.

On the other hand, there is an interesting school of thought that postulates that population pressure may indeed provide the stimulus for progress. Boserup, in the course of her extensive anthropological studies, provides evidence supporting the hypothesis that population pressure brought about a progressive intensification in agricultural technology, which has helped not only to expand food production but also provide employment. The quest for improved agricultural technology and the ushering in of the Green Revolution in India are also directly related to the compulsions generated by population pressure. It is true that the Green Revolution has lost its initial impetus but the lessons learnt therefrom could help maintain sustained and widespread improvement in farming practices and thus promote continued increase in food production.

In a similar way, population growth instead of promoting poverty and widespread unemployment as is conventionally believed, may actually generate a movement towards reduction of socio-economic disparities. Urbanisation, industrialisation, education and improvement in communications and transport in the coming decades may make the poor segments of the population keenly alive to the magnitude of their deprivation; this in turn may generate social pressures which will make the current socio-economic disparities untenable. Should this happen, and the bulk of the population be actually involved in productive employment, then a situation will arise in which people, instead of being viewed as 'problems and liabilities', will be looked upon as 'opportunities and assets'.

It is a hard reality that, in spite of heroic efforts at fertility control including such measures as compulsory sterilisation after the third child, the populations of many developing countries will continue to rise and double in the next three or four decades, unless catastrophes of the kind indicated by pessimistic predictions overtake them. The sensible course would seem to lie in vigorous implementation of corrective actions to arrest population growth, to generate productive employment and to intensify food production using the latest and most advanced technology available, and to hope that the optimistic predictions of the Boserup school will ultimately prevail.

REFERENCES

Boserup, E. (1965). *The Conditions of Agricultural Growth: The Economics of Agrarian Change under Population Pressure*, George and Unwin Ltd, London.
Economic Commission for South Asia and Far East (1973). *Economic Survey of South Asia and Far East* 1972, pp. 91–95, United Nations, Bangkok.
Malthus, Thomas Robert (1798). *Essay on the Principle of Population*.
Porter, A. (1889). *The Diseases of the Madras Famine of* 1877–79, Madras.
Swaminathan, M. S. (1973). *Sardar Patel Memorial Lecture*, p. 3, All India Radio, New Delhi.
Swaminathan, M. S. (1973). *Malthus and Mendel, Silver Jubiless Commemoration Lecture*, Indian National Science Academy.

PART 2

NUTRITIONAL REQUIREMENTS AND NATIONAL POLICIES

CHAPTER 5

Protein and energy requirements of the UK as part of the World Community

R. G. WHITEHEAD

MRC Dunn Nutrition Unit, Cambridge

In this paper I will be discussing recent views on protein and energy requirements with special reference to their relevance for the UK and its position within a rapidly changing world community. I conclude by indicating how, if international economic constraints force us to, we could modify our dietary protein intake, particularly of animal protein, and still satisfy our requirements with an adequate margin of safety.

It is an unfortunate fact of life that most of the world cannot, and perhaps never will be able to, enjoy the same protein intake that we receive in the UK. If this were not the case we would not need to be so obsessed by protein requirements. During the past 15 years or so numerous national and international expert committees have met with the basic aim of defining the minimum safe level for protein and energy. However, the promotion and maintenance of health can never be the sole consideration in the deliberations of such committees; the economic feasibility of meeting any recommendation has always had to be taken into account. During a visit to Guatemala in 1967, for example, I was told that the National Research Council (NRC, 1964) recommended nutrient allowances for protein, being used there as a dietary target, would not be achieved even if all the financial resources of that country were directed towards obtaining protein-rich foods for the people. The problem for Guatemala was the same for most other developing countries; the need to define truly adequate minimum physiological protein requirements was an obvious priority.

Trends in recommended allowances over recent years are summarised in Table 1. It will be seen that while estimated energy requirements have altered little, those for protein have been falling steadily and are now much lower than they used to be in 1964. One effect of these changes has been that the 'protein gap' no longer looms so large in our planning: indeed, many nutritionists feel that the 'energy gap' is a better description of the problem in most developing countries.

47

TABLE 1

CHANGES DURING THE PAST 30 YEARS IN THE MINIMUM DAILY AMOUNTS OF PROTEIN (g/kg BODYWEIGHT) AND ENERGY (kJ/kg BODYWEIGHT) WHICH HAVE BEEN CONSIDERED SATISFACTORY FOR THE HEALTH AND GROWTH OF YOUNG CHILDREN

(Based on Whitehead, 1973)

Year	Energy	Protein	Protein/energy ratio (%)	References
1941, 1945, 1948	418 (100)	3·3	13·2	NRC (1948)
1963	418 (100)	2·5	10·0	NRC (1964)
1965	—	1·5	—	FAO/WHO (1965)
1968	385 (92)	2·1	9·1	NRC (1968)
1969	439 (105)	1·7	6·5	DHSS (1969)
1973	424 (101)	1·5	5·9	FAO/WHO (1973)

Calculated on the basis of an average UK diet. Values in parentheses are the kcal equivalents of kJ data.

PRESENT DAY PROTEIN CONSUMPTION IN THE UK

What is the significance of this to a country such as ours? Table 2 shows the intake of protein and energy per person in households of differing economic circumstances for the year ended July–September 1975 (Ministry of Agriculture, Fisheries and Food, 1976). Using the guidelines laid down by the Department of Health and Social Security (1969), it appears that, on the basis of assumed physiological requirements, households in all sectors of the community are purchasing for consumption almost twice the minimum amount of protein needed. Even using a second more conservative guideline in which it is reasoned that a culturally acceptable UK diet needs to contain at least 10% of its energy as protein, there is an apparent excess of 25% in protein intake.

This type of information is, of course, not new; it has been known for many years that people in the more affluent countries are consuming quantities of protein of this magnitude. Until recently, when this has been questioned the usual response has been the retort 'so what!'—it is our cultural tradition to eat in this way and there is no evidence whatsoever to indicate that a protein intake at this level confers any health disadvantage. But this attitude, like so many others in our rapidly changing world, is having to be modified and for diverse reasons. One question which is asked is whether, in view of the high cost of food, the average family will continue to be able to afford so much protein, particularly animal protein.

Other, more internationally minded people, are concerned with the morality of intensive meat production. Grain which could be fed to malnourished communities in the developing countries is apparently being used by us to produce a nutritionally unnecessary large amount of meat.

TABLE 2

NUTRITIONAL VALUE OF HOUSEHOLD FOOD IN DIFFERENT INCOME GROUPS DURING
JULY–SEPTEMBER 1975

(Ministry of Agriculture, Fisheries and Food, 1976)

	Household income per week				Old age pensioners
	£82 and above	£49–82	£28–49	£28 and less	
Intake per person per day					
Energy (MJ)	2 280	2 240	2 330	2 370	2 520
(kcal)	9·5	9·4	9·7	9·9	10·5
Protein (g)	73·9	71·0	71·7	75·6	75·6
% of recommended intake					
Energy	97	95	95	99	110
Protein					
(a) if protein/energy ratio was 10%	126	120	117	127	132
(b) on minimum requirement	191	186	182	189	190

An arbitrary 10% is made to allow for wastage. This is the standard MAFF practice.

Political economists are forced to query whether, in the light of developments in world politics, the affluent countries will continue to be able to corner a disproportionately large share of the world's protein production.

SAFE LEVELS OF PROTEIN INTAKE

How much protein is necessary for health is thus just as much a strategic problem for us in Europe as it is for an African or Asian country and this raises the important issue of how sure we can be of our estimated requirements for health. Perhaps there is a slight difference in emphasis in the approach to this problem by industrial and developing countries. Even the relatively low values for protein now being suggested as safe by FAO/WHO

(1973) could bring about an *increase* in protein consumption in most developing countries if they became target intakes for a national food policy. Should future research indicate they were not completely safe, the situation would still have been *improved* if the target were met. It would be a quite different matter, however, if economic circumstances forced a European country like the UK to contemplate the introduction of a tighter dietary policy. If the estimated safe levels which were adopted for planning purposes proved ill based, this could result in the *reintroduction* of protein deficiency into this country. It is, however, obviously desirable for the welfare of both developing and industrialised countries that there should be no doubt about such an important issue.

The data in Table 1 indicate that the protein–energy ratio of the type of diet eaten in the UK could fall to as low as 5·9% even in a one year old child before there was any risk of protein deficiency, assuming of course that energy intake was maintained to satisfy requirement. The data available to the FAO/WHO (1973) committee seemed to justify this conclusion, but there was one disclaimer, Dr R. Passmore of Edinburgh, who expressed the following contrary opinion:

'There is no evidence that such a protein derived energy is compatible with a healthy vigorous life: in the diets of healthy communities 10% or more of the energy is provided by protein. It is possible that epidemiological studies on the continued use of low protein diets might uncover metabolic changes that were not detectable in the short term studies on which the safe levels recommended by the committee were based.'

Passmore produced no factual evidence to support his case, however, either then or since, and by and large the FAO/WHO (1973) safe levels have found general acceptance among the scientific community. At the same time, it has been recognised that these estimates were based on a rather small amount of primary data and various workers, including Inoue, *et al.* (1973), Calloway (1975) and Scrimshaw (1976) have attempted to provide the necessary extra information.

The FAO/WHO (1973) estimates were based partly on the factorial method of estimation, which is a summation of the amounts of nitrogen needed to replace obligatory losses in the urine, faeces and sweat, together with the extra nitrogen required for growth, pregnancy, lactation, etc., but extensive use was also made of available nitrogen balance data.

The committee would in fact have preferred to base all their estimates on nitrogen balance data, but in many age groups none were available, particularly on individuals fed exclusively egg or milk proteins. These have become recognised as the standard proteins for this purpose. The committee were thus forced to estimate nitrogen balance from data on obligatory nitrogen losses. In the few cases where relevant nitrogen balance data were available, calculated obligatory losses multiplied by a mean factor of 1·3 seemed to provide a reasonable estimate and this factor was adopted for all age groups except children under 1 year. In addition, an allowance was made for protein quality in different types of diet, and a further allowance was made to cover known variations in the protein requirements of different individuals. The value which theoretically would cover the requirements of 97·5% of the population was called the safe level.

The validity of these estimates is clearly dependent on various assumptions including the adequacy or otherwise of relatively few nitrogen balance studies and on the use of the 1·3 factor. Carrying out accurate balance studies, particularly over an extended period of time, is incredibly difficult and requires special research facilities which are all too frequently unavailable. In the UK, for example, there are no really adequate facilities for this purpose at all. I am sure that this is the reason why, in spite of its critical international importance, so few attempts have been made to provide the extra information needed to develop the reasoning of the FAO/WHO (1973) committee.

The few criticisms which have been made of the FAO/WHO (1973) estimates for protein have mostly centred around the well-known interrelationship between energy intake and the efficiency of nitrogen utilisation. When a diet contains relatively little protein, more energy is required to maintain nitrogen balance, and vice versa. Scrimshaw (1976) has claimed that most of the nitrogen balance studies used by the FAO/WHO (1973) committee were carried out under conditions in which energy intake was in excess of the physiological needs of the subjects. In other words, such levels of protein would only satisfy nitrogen balance under conditions which might also lead to obesity. The fact that the 'safe' level of egg or milk protein, when fed with a level of energy appropriate to the energy needs of a specific individual, is often inadequate to cover his needs for nitrogen balance is obvious from the work of Calloway (1975), Inoue, et al. (1973), as well as that of the Massachusetts Institute of Technology (MIT) group, Garza, et al. (1976). The MIT group have also fed the safe level of protein to young volunteers for periods of up to three months. Many could not achieve nitrogen balance and even showed biochemical signs of muscle or liver abnormality or both, which needed a considerable excess of energy to alleviate.

Furthermore, when proteins of inferior quality were used, the subjects had even more difficulty in maintaining nitrogen balance, even after the customary allowance for protein quality had been made. This, of course, also casts doubt on the validity of using the 1·3 factor for calculating nitrogen balance from obligatory nitrogen loss data (Scrimshaw, 1976).

These criticisms are based on very few data, but so were the original recommendations. I have mentioned them because they do illustrate the fact that we know too little at the present time to be dogmatic about safe intakes of protein. The present calculated levels are valuable for what has been termed diagnostic purposes, by which is meant the interpretation of dietary intake data; but there is, I believe, too big an area of doubt to make actual recommendations about protein requirements with absolute confidence. An expert committee can only make a critical and informed judgement on the basis of available information. Where it is thought that such information may be inadequate, it is the responsibility of the scientific community to keep an open mind and be prepared to revise their opinions if this should be justified by new data.

PROTEIN NEEDS IN THE UK IN COMING YEARS

These comments clearly have a direct bearing on the main topic of this meeting and explain why I am not prepared to make an unqualified statement on how much we could allow international, social and economic constraints to affect dietary protein consumption in the UK without this adversely affecting the nutrient needs of the people. If I must 'come off the fence' and make some comment, it can only be a rather conservative one.

In any country, unless there is an efficient routine nutritional health monitoring service which can detect early signs of malnutrition in every potentially 'at risk' segment of the population, one must have a diet, the composition of which is adequate to cover the needs of everyone in the community regardless of age, sex, occupation, physiological status, etc. Such a diet is clearly wasteful; it provides nutrients too generously for most people, but it does ensure that if a person satisfies his energy needs then he will not be short of other essential nutrients.

The age groups with the need for the highest dietary protein concentration are those for young children. We must assume that by one year of age, many children will be living on a diet which is largely based on the adult fare, and it is thus their requirements which will determine the safe concentration of protein in a diet. Furthermore, I have indicated that the adequacy of a protein intake is dependent on the associated intake of dietary energy. We must, therefore, also take into account those one year old children who have a low physiological need for energy, either because they have an especially efficient metabolism or because they are relatively inactive. As Waterlow and Payne (1975) have calculated, it is highly unlikely on this basis that any one year old child will need a diet in which the theoretical protein/energy ratio is greater than 6·5% or, say, 9·5%, when corrected for the average protein quality of a mixed diet in the UK. It would, I suggest, be reasonable to use this figure for emergency planning purposes if the food supply situation ever became serious enough to warrant such an extreme step. It is, in fact, remarkably similar to the 10% figure adopted by the DHSS panel on recommended nutrient allowances in 1969.

If we re-examine the present-day National Food Survey data in Table 2 in relation to the DHSS (1969) 10% value, it is apparent that average protein consumption within the home is around 20% above this level, and if other meals are taken into account the difference would be greater still. We could certainly allow our overall protein intake to drop by this amount without any conceivable risk of protein deficiency.

If it ever became necessary to make such changes to our diet, what sort of food would we be eating? It would not necessarily involve too serious an alteration in our dietary habits, more a reversal of recent trends in consumption towards the type of food which might have been eaten by our parents or grandparents, say 50–100 years ago. Two major changes since that time have been a gradual reduction in our consumption of potatoes and cereal based foods. We now eat less bread and jam, for example, less bread with our meat, we make fewer meat and potato dishes like hot pots and stews, etc.

In Table 3 I show what would happen if we cut our meat consumption by about two thirds and made up for this by eating more bread and potatoes. A small cut in milk, cream and cheese has also been made, but on the assumption we might need more jam and margarine or butter to eat with our bread I have increased these items slightly. These calculations are based on Ministry of Agriculture, Fisheries and Food (1975) data published in the National Food Survey for the year 1973.

In Table 4 the nutrient content of the 'emergency' dietary pattern is compared with that of our present diet. The fall in animal protein is partly made up by increased vegetable protein intake, but the diet now has a protein:energy ratio of 10% rather than 12%. Total fat intake is down, too. The remaining nutrients are little affected. Carbohydrate intake would be elevated somewhat and only iron, vitamin D and ribo-flavin might be causes for concern. The former two are already covered by the fortification of bread and margarine; this could be increased if it were thought necessary. Riboflavin is added to breakfast cereals and it could be added to other cereal foods or milk to avoid any possibility of deficiency.

There are obviously other ways of manipulating our present diet; for most nutrients there is plenty of leeway. I emphasise these are suggestions about what *could* be done. Perhaps it is, however, comforting that dietary doom is not just round the corner, at least not for the immediate future.

TABLE 3

CONTRIBUTIONS MADE BY GROUPS OF FOODS TO THE DAILY PROTEIN AND ENERGY VALUE OF HOUSEHOLD FOOD DURING 1973 PER PERSON[a] MODIFIED TO PRODUCE A DIETARY PATTERN WITH A PROTEIN/ENERGY RATIO OF 10%

Groups of Foods	1973 diet				Emergency diet			
	Energy (kJ)	Energy (kcal)	Protein (g)	Protein/energy ratio (%)	Energy (kJ)	Energy (kcal)	Protein (g)	Protein/energy ratio (%)
Milk, cream and cheese	1 460	349	17·9	20·5	1 255	300	15·4	—
Meat	1 635	391	19·5	19·9	481	115	5·7	—
Fish	105	25	2·9	46·4	105	25	2·9	—
Eggs	188	45	3·7	32·9	188	45	3·7	—
Edible fats and oils	1 485	355	0·1	0·1	1 883	450	0·1	—
Sugar and preserves	1 029	246	0·0	0·0	1 255	300	0·0	—
Potatoes	448	107	2·8	10·5	837	200	5·3	—
Other vegetables	318	76	3·8	20·0	318	76	3·8	—
Fruit	243	58	0·7	4·8	243	58	0·7	—
Bread and flour	1 732	414	13·8	13·3	2 092	500	16·6	—
Other cereal foods	1 171	280	4·9	7·0	1 171	280	4·9	—
Beverages	38	9	0·2	8·9	38	9	0·2	—
Other foods	176	42	1·0	9·5	176	42	1·0	—
Total	10 042	2 400	71·4	11·9	10 042	2 400	60·3	10·0

[a] Source: Ministry of Agriculture, Fisheries and Food (1975).

TABLE 4

NUTRITIONAL VALUE OF THE 1973 HOUSEHOLD FOOD PATTERN[a] IN COMPARISON WITH THE 'EMERGENCY DIET'

Diet	Energy (MJ)	(kcal)	Protein (g)	Fat (g)	Carbo-hydrate (g)	Calcium (mg)	Iron (mg)	Thiamin (mg)	Ribo-flavin (mg)	Nicotinic acid (equiva-lents) (mg)	Vitamin C (mg)	Vitamin A (retinol equivalents) (μg)	Vitamin D (μg)
								Composition					
1973	10	2 400	71·4	111	293	1 020	12·7	1·22	1·79	29·0	53	1 270	2·89
Emergency	10	2 400	60·3	96	342	963	11·7	1·21	1·51	24·6	63	1 104	3·15
						Adequacy[b]							
1973	104	104	124 (190)[c]	—	—	193	118	134	132	193	189	190	89
Emergency	104	104	105 (160)[c]	—	—	182	109	133	111	164	225	165	97

[a] Source: Ministry of Agriculture, Fisheries and Food.
[b] On the basis of Department of Health and Social Security, 1969.
[c] Values in parentheses based on minimum requirements (Department of Health and Social Security, 1969).

REFERENCES

Calloway, D. H. (1975). *J. Nutr.*, **105**, 914.
Department of Health and Social Security (1969). *Recommended Intakes of Nutrients for the United Kingdom*, Reports on Public Health and Medical Subjects, No. 120, HMSO, London.
FAO/WHO (1965). *Protein Requirements*, FAO Nutr. Mtg Rep. Ser., No. 37, and Wld. Hlth. Org. techn. Rep. Ser., No. 301.
FAO/WHO (1973). *Energy and Protein Requirements*, FAO Nutr. Mtg Rep. Ser., No. 52 and Wld. Hlth Org. techn. Rep. Ser., No. 522.
Garza, C., Young, V. I. and Scrimshaw, N. S. (1976). *J. Nutr.* In press.
Inoue, G., Fugita, Y. and Niiyama, Y. (1973). *J. Nutr.*, **103**, 1673.
Ministry of Agriculture, Fisheries and Food (1975). *Household Food Composition and Expenditure:* 1973, HMSO, London.
Ministry of Agriculture, Fisheries and Food (1976). *Food Facts No. 1, January*, MAFF Press Office, London.
NRC (1948). *Recommended Dietary Allowances*, Reprint and Circular Series No. 129, National Research Council, Washington, D.C.
NRC (1964). *Recommended Dietary Allowances*, Publication 1146, National Academy of Sciences, National Research Council, Washington, D.C.
NRC (1968). *Recommended Dietary Allowances*, Publication 1694, National Academy of Sciences, National Research Council, Washington, D.C.
Scrimshaw, N. S. (1976). *New Engl. J. Med.*, **294**, 198.
Waterlow, J. C. and Payne, P. R. (1975). *Nature, Lond.*, **258**, 113.
Whitehead, R. G. (1973). In *Proteins in Human Nutrition*, p. 103, edited by J. W. G. Porter and B. A. Rolls, Academic Press, New York and London.

CHAPTER 6

Some micronutrients that may be critical

A. S. TRUSWELL

Queen Elizabeth College, London

Dr Whitehead (Chapter 5) has dealt with energy and protein, the components which necessitate the bulk of food. For a man to obtain 2700 kcal (11·3 MJ) requires 680 g/day of food in weight if the energy density is 4 kcal/g, and the present corresponding official protein recommendation is 68 g/day. I am left to consider all the other essential nutrients that are required in amounts from 4 g down to about 2 μg (Table 1). I chose the word 'micronutrient' for my title to avoid separating vitamins from essential elements, which is unhelpful in practical nutrition, and to emphasise that if the diet is lacking in any of these substances we have the options (if we want) of mixing some of it into a food during manufacture or of taking tablets from the chemist, without altering the weight of food in our shopping basket.

In the United Nations system the Food and Agriculture Organization sees itself as responsible for trying to improve and safeguard the bulk of food, with its energy and calories, while it leaves the World Health Organization to deal with all the other nutrients. This is sensible because recognition, prevention and treatment of micronutrient deficiency often involves medical and health personnel and medical measures. A similar division of responsibility between ministries of agriculture and of health operates in most countries including, I think, our own. The size of some of the requirements in the lowest two lines of Table 1 are rather large to fit the name 'micronutrient' very well but we need a name for this whole group. So far no one has suggested a better word.

The 28 nutrients in Table 1 are all established as essential for man. Human deficiency disease has been reported and confirmed for all except four or five if we include calcium in this category. Taking these in turn, calcium is obviously essential to form and replace bone and for its important roles in soft tissues, though it is difficult to find a clear picture of human deficiency. Pantothenic acid, manganese and molybdenum are specific components of coenzyme A, pyruvate carboxylase and xanthine oxidase respectively; animals on diets deficient in any of these develop disease. Fluoride has recently been found to be essential for normal growth and reproduction in rats (Schwartz and Milne, 1972); the

57

Department of Health and Social Security (1969) recommends bringing water up to 1 ppm if it is naturally low in fluoride as a measure to reduce dental caries. The Royal College of Physicians: Committee on Fluoridation of Water Supplies (1976) agrees that this level of intake is beneficial and safe; Wretlind (1975) includes fluoride in recommendations for total parenteral nutrition and it is in the new table of recommended dietary intakes for West Germany (Deutsche Gesellschaft für Ernährung, 1975).

TABLE 1

DAILY REQUIREMENTS OF ESSENTIAL NUTRIENTS FOR MAN

Adult daily requirement	Essential nutrients for man
2–10 μg	vitamin D; vitamin B_{12}; chromium
circa 100 μg	biotin; iodine; vitamin K; molybdenum
200–400 μg	folate
circa 1 mg	vitamin A; thiamin; riboflavin; pyridoxine; iron; copper
5–10 mg	manganese; pantothenate
circa 15 mg	nicotinic acid; vitamin E; zinc; iron; vitamin C
300 mg	magnesium
circa 1 g	calcium; phosphorus
1–5 g	sodium; chloride; potassium; essential fatty acids

For anyone who feels that the names in Table 1 have been around a long time I think it is worth pointing out that human deficiency disease for eight or nine of these have been discovered since the Second World War (Table 2).

Pyridoxine deficiency was first described in 1953 (Snyderman, et al.) and 1954 (Coursin); the features of magnesium deficiency were worked out in the late 1950s (Flink, et al., 1954; Hanna, et al., 1960); essential fatty acid (EFA) deficiency was first reported about 1957 (Hansen, et al.) but has only become well established since 1971 (Collins, et al.). Knowledge of the relation between biotin and seborrhoeic dermatitis in infants has been growing slowly since 1950 (Svejcar and Homolka). Zinc deficiency was first reported in 1963 (Prasad, et al.) but not well established until 1972 (Halsted, et al.); copper deficiency was first described about 1964 (Cordano, et al.) but not clearly delineated until 1971 (Al Rashid and Spangler). Vitamin E deficiency in premature infants was first reported about 1966 (Hassan, et al.) but it has taken a few years for confirmation and general acceptance of the syndrome. Perhaps the first clear cut description of human phosphate deficiency (induced by aluminium antacids) appeared in 1968 (Lotz, et al.). Chromium deficiency was first reported in animals in 1959 (Schwarz and Mertz) and in children in 1968 (Hopkins, *et al.*).

The 1969 edition of a standard textbook (Davidson and Passmore) does not mention chromium. Of three other nutrients it says 'So far there is no unequivocal proof that vitamin E deficiency ever occurs in man', and 'So far there is no evidence that dietary deficiency of copper ever occurs in man', and 'satisfactory scientific proof that EFA deficiency

TABLE 2
DISCOVERY OF HUMAN DEFICIENCY SYNDROMES

Pyridoxine	1953 (Snyderman, *et al.*), 1954 (Coursin)
Magnesium	1954 (Flink, *et al.*), 1960 (Hanna, *et al.*)
Essential fatty acids	1957 (A. E. Hansen, *et al.*), 1971 (Collins, *et al.*)
Biotin	Related to seborrhoeic dermatitis of infants, 1950 (Svejcar and Homolka)
Zinc	1963 (Prasad, *et al.*), 1972 (Halsted, *et al.*)
Copper	1964 (Cordano, *et al.*), 1971 (Al Rashid and Spangler)
Vitamin E	1966 (Hassan, *et al.*)
Phosphate	1968 (Lotz, *et al.*)
Chromium	1968 (Hopkins, *et al.*)

exists in man is still lacking'. This edition was published the same year as the present British Recommended Intakes of Nutrients. We live in interesting times and certainly in nutrition the list of micronutrients which are definitely required by man has continued to grow at a time when some have mistakenly supposed that there are no challenges remaining in this branch of science.

In addition to the substances in Table 1, other elements have been shown in recent years, by using special isolator systems and plastic cages, to be essential for small laboratory animals. These are selenium, vanadium, nickel, tin and silicon. Human deficiencies have not been discovered and except for selenium (which is a rare element, not uniformly distributed) are perhaps unlikely to occur because of the abundance of most of these elements.

This list does not include cobalt because this metal appears to be needed only in the single organic form of vitamin B_{12} in non-ruminants. It does not include sulphur either because the requirement for the essential sulphur amino acids certainly provides the sulphur needed to synthesise such compounds in the body as glutathione and chondroitin sulphate. Thiamin and biotin both contain sulphur too.

Such substances as choline, inositol and para-aminobenzoic acid, that appear in older books, are not on my list of nutrients essential for man.

With others of historical interest they have fallen by the wayside. Choline, for example, is handled quite differently by rats compared with man. Rats have considerable choline oxidase activity in their livers but humans do not (Kensler and Langermann, 1954).

Returning to the list of definitely essential nutrients, can we put them in some sort of rank order of importance?

On the world scale
It is WHO policy that the four nutritional diseases deserving the highest priority are protein-calorie malnutrition, xerophthalmia, nutritional anaemias and endemic goitre. In some more limited areas beriberi, pellagra or rickets warrant local priority, but scurvy is uncommon (WHO, 1972; Bengoa, 1973). In other words, after protein and energy, deficiencies of vitamin A, iron (and folic acid) and iodine are of global importance; thiamin, niacin and vitamin D deficiencies are of local importance and vitamin C deficiency is uncommon.

Dietary intakes in Britain
In the recent reports of the National Food Survey intakes appear possibly critical for three nutrients. Table 3 shows nutrients as percentages of recommended intakes in families with two adults and numbers of children ranging from none to four or more. The intakes of vitamin D and of iron

TABLE 3

NUTRITIONAL VALUE OF HOUSEHOLD FOOD CONSUMPTION[a] AS A PERCENTAGE OF RECOMMENDED INTAKE[b]

| No. of children | Two Adults and | | | | |
	0	1	2	3	4 or more
Energy	101	95	88	89	87
Protein	130	119	109	115	106
(in terms of minimum requirement)	196	182	170	180	167
Calcium	206	185	174	167	161
Iron	116	106	93	96	91
Thiamin	125	120	114	120	126
Riboflavin	123	130	124	135	128
Nicotinic acid equivalent	187	184	172	189	178
Vitamin C	190	197	159	152	134
Vitamin A	206	219	187	190	164
Vitamin D	110	71	67	61	63

[a] Source: Ministry of Agriculture, Fisheries and Food (1975).
[b] Source: Department of Health and Social Security (1969).

fall well below 100% when there are four or more children in the family. Vitamin C also shows a steep gradient and the figure in families with four or more children seems to leave little margin because there is a marked seasonal variation of ascorbic acid intake and it is sensitive to destruction during food processing and preparation. The vitamin D requirements can, of course, be provided by exposure of the skin to sunlight but we cannot rely on this in the winter or in, for instance, Asian girls.

Incidentally, intakes of nutrients appear to be most critical at present in the UK in families with four or more children, even with two parents. By contrast the National Food Survey shows better intakes of the critical nutrients in low socio-economic groups and in old age pensioners. I believe it is our responsibility to bring these facts to the attention of those in the government responsible for food and financial policies.

However only eight micronutrients are calculated for the National Food Survey (and these from food tables). These are the nutrients which appear along with energy and protein in the main table of the Department of Health and Social Security (1969) report on *Recommended Intakes of Nutrients*. If intake of one of the other nutrients in Table 1 had become too low, we should not know about it from this source.

Deficiency disease in Britain
This is not uncommon from deficiency of vitamin D, iron and folate.

Rickets and osteomalacia have continued to occur since they 'reappeared' around 1963 (Arneil and Crosbie). Six or more articles reporting varying numbers of cases have appeared in the medical journals annually in recent years. *The Lancet* (Anon., 1973) considers that vitamin D deficiency is 'a problem of our time which merits urgent attention' and I believe this view is taken in the Department of Health and Social Security. Infants, Asian girls, the elderly and patients who have had gastric surgery or have to take anticonvulsants are at special risk.

Iron deficiency anaemia affects around 10% of women and a smaller proportion of men (Callender, 1973b). Precise numbers must depend on the criteria used and the segment of the population sampled. Susceptibility to iron deficiency depends chiefly on two phenomena. Menstrual losses average some 20 ml of blood but range up to 500 ml (Hallberg, 1966). It is very difficult for those with requirements at the upper end of this distribution to meet them with our cereal based mixed diets cooked in aluminium pots. Hallberg (1975) sees the almost universal prevalence of iron deficiency as a consequence of changing from the hunting way of life, which has not (yet) been solved by natural selection.

Folate deficiency shows itself principally as megaloblastic anaemia of pregnancy, which has occurred in about 2·5% of women in recent British reports (Giles and Shuttleworth, 1958; Hibbard, 1964; Varadi, *et al.*, 1966; Willoughby, 1967). Milder grades of folate deficiency, as indicated by early megaloblastic changes in the bone marrow (Beaven, *et al.*, 1966; Temperley, *et al.*, 1968) and low concentrations of folate in plasma and red cells (Varadi, *et al.*, 1966) occur in around 25% of pregnant women. Occasional cases of folate-responsive megaloblastic anaemia have been reported in premature infants (Hoffbrand, 1970), in non-pregnant Asian women (Britt, *et al.*, 1971) and in patients taking certain drugs which can interfere with folate metabolism—anticonvulsants, antimalarials, cotrimoxazole, alcohol, methotrexate and possibly oral contraceptives (Truswell, 1973). Low serum folate concentrations were found in some 15% of men and women over 65 years of age in the Department of Health and Social Security (1972) survey of the elderly. Folate deficiency with pancytopenia and megaloblastic marrow has lately been reported in patients receiving intensive therapy after surgery or trauma with measures including dialysis or intravenous amino acid/ethanol solutions (Wardrop, *et al.*, 1975; Ibbotson, *et al.*, 1975).

Deficiencies of four other nutrients are occasionally seen in Britain. Iodide deficiency could be the commonest of these. In 1966 the West Derbyshire Medical Society reported 'We had thought that we might be writing a footnote to history in forecasting the imminent passing of Derbyshire neck but with a quarter of the thyroid abnormalities (totalling 7·7% of the women) in the 20–39 age group, that time has obviously not yet come.'

Scurvy affects mostly infants and elderly people. Brook (1973) has reviewed the cases reported between 1958 and 1971; these total 165 but there are clearly others which do not get written up. The Department of Health and Social Security (1972) survey of the elderly encountered two cases during the examination of 879 representative individuals. Low leucocyte ascorbic acid can occur in as many as 30% of elderly men at the end of winter (Milne, *et al.*, 1971).

Thiamin deficiency in all its forms continues to surprise doctors when they see it—beriberi heart disease (Byrne-Quinn and Fessas, 1969; Carney, 1971) even the shoshin form (McIntyre and Stanley, 1971) also Wernicke's encephalopathy (Philip and Smith, 1973) and combined cardiomyopathy plus encephalopathy (Baron and Oliver, 1958). Most of these patients had been consuming much alcohol and little food.

Dietary vitamin B_{12} deficiency is rare but nowadays most likely to be seen in Hindu women often in relation to pregnancy (Stewart, *et al.*, 1970; Roberts, *et al.*, 1973) rather than in British vegans.

Two of the above ways of deciding which are the important or critical micronutrients are contrasted in Table 4. While vitamin A and nicotinic acid deficiencies give great and moderate concern respectively to WHO (left hand column) they do not occur in Britain except as rare complications of certain medical conditions. This absence of vitamin A and nicotinic acid deficiencies now extends throughout Europe and can be linked, at least partly, to the rarity of primary dietary protein deficiency.

The right hand column of Table 4 shows the nutrients (other than protein and energy) for which there are recommended daily intakes in the main table of the Department of Health and Social Security (1969) report. If we were to have a system of nutrition labelling of food products based on these recommended intakes, people might go shopping for good intakes of vitamin A of which they do not need any more, and not know about

TABLE 4

NUTRITIONAL DEFICIENCY DISEASE IN BRITAIN

Deficiency disease on world scale	Deficiency disease occurs in UK	Recommended intake[a]
Vitamin A	—	Vitamin A
Iodine	Iodine	—
Iron	Iron	Iron
Folate	Folate	—
Vitamin D	Vitamin D	Vitamin D
Nicotinic acid	—	Nicotinic acid
Thiamin	Thiamin	Thiamin
Vitamin C	Vitamin C	Vitamin C
—	Vitamin B_{12}	—

[a] Source: Department of Health and Social Security (1969).

folic acid which they might need. There is a good reason why iodine and folic acid do not have recommended intakes: it is very difficult to predict how much of these two nutrients is contained in individual foods. The amount of iodine in foods depends on the iodine in the soil and water on which they are grown. And folic acid occurs in foods in many different forms. In a single food Osborn-White and Smith (1973) demonstrated 14 different forms, derivatives and conjugates of folic acid with up to seven glutamate residues in sheep's liver. The pattern appears to vary in different foods. Monoglutamates or 'free' folate are well absorbed, but enough human experiments have not yet been done to test the absorption of different polyglutamates in a variety of people and conditions.

We need to have biologically useful values for folate in our food tables so that we can have corresponding recommended dietary intakes. In a meeting on nutrition at the Royal Society of Medicine early in 1976 one speaker said that folic acid deficiency is the commonest vitamin deficiency in the world.

Another difficulty that can arise from relying on the official recommended intakes is illustrated by a complaint about an advertisement which was ultimately sent to me for an opinion. The advert reads 'Although certain minerals and vitamins have to be reduced in the milling of wheat into white flour, they are added to the flour *after* milling—as a legal requirement in fact—to maintain the nutrient level of your bread.' Now although certain nutrients—calcium, iron and thiamin—are added back as required by the Food Standards Committee (1974a) to safeguard the nation's nutrition, the complainants were right that other nutrients are reduced and not added back, such as riboflavin, niacin, pyridoxine, folic acid, vitamin E, chromium, zinc, fat, fibre, etc. These are mostly nutrients without official recommended intakes. Before we condemn the complainants as obsessed with unimportant minor nutrients let us look at the new lists of recommended intakes in other advanced countries. The latest USA tables contain 16 nutrients and the West German 20 (Table 5).

TABLE 5

RECOMMENDED DIETARY INTAKES

USA (1974)[a]	UK (1969)	W. Germany (1975)
Vitamin A	Vitamin A	Vitamin A
Vitamin D	Vitamin D	Vitamin D
Vitamin E	—	Vitamin E
Ascorbic acid	Ascorbic acid	Vitamin C
Folacin	—	Folic acid
Niacin	Nicotinic acid	Niacin
Riboflavin	Riboflavin	Riboflavin
Thiamin	Thiamin	Thiamin
Vitamin B_6	—	Vitamin B_6
Vitamin B_{12}	—	Vitamin B_{12}
Calcium	Calcium	Calcium
Phosphorus	—	Phosphorus
Iodine	—	Iodine
Iron	Iron	Iron
Magnesium	—	Magnesium
Zinc	—	—
		Pantothenic acid
		Sodium
		Chloride
		Potassium
		Fluoride

[a] And Canada (1974).

Might some of these newer essential nutrients turn out to be important?
Pyridoxine is coenzyme for over 60 different enzyme systems. Most of these
are on the pathways of amino acid metabolism and include transaminases,
decarboxylases that produce amines and also γ-aminobutyric acid in the
brain, enzymes involved in conversion of tryptophan to nicotinamide and
in haem synthesis. There are several different deficiency syndromes, such
as convulsions, hypochromic sideroblastic anaemia, peripheral neuropathy
or tongue and lip lesions. The body stores only a small amount of pyridoxine; several drugs are antagonists, *e.g.* isoniazid, and pyridoxine
metabolism is disturbed in pregnancy and in women taking oral
contraceptives.
    Adams, *et al.* (1973) reported from St. Mary's Hospital, London, that
in 22 depressed women whose symptoms were judged to be due to the
effects of oral contraceptives 11 showed biochemical evidence of an
absolute deficiency of pyridoxine and their symptoms responded to 20 mg
pyridoxine hydrochloride twice daily in a double blind trial. Plasma
pyridoxal phosphate falls in pregnancy (Shane and Contractor, 1975)
and in rheumatoid arthritis (Schumacher, *et al.*, 1975). It has been reported
that glucose tolerance improved after large doses of pyridoxine in women
with gestational diabetes (Coelingh Bennink and Schreurs, 1975).
    Zinc deficiency has been clearly established in Egypt and Iran. It
produces a picture of dwarfism with sexual infantilism in teenage boys and
girls (Halsted, *et al.*, 1972). Coming nearer home, zinc deficiency has been
found in association with a variety of diseases such as malabsorption,
burns, alcoholism and chronic alcoholism. In such patients delayed wound
healing responds to treatment with zinc. The rare inherited disease,
acrodermatitis enteropathica has recently been found to respond to large
doses of zinc. This was discovered in London (Moynahan, 1974).
    But most surprising of all zinc-responsive growth failure has been
reported in young children from middle-class homes in Denver, Colorado,
USA. The children had impaired taste acuity, poor appetite and reduced
hair zinc. Dietary histories showed that they had been eating little meat.
They improved markedly when given daily supplements of 0·4–0·8 mg
zinc/kg (Hambidge, *et al.*, 1972). Good dietary sources of zinc are meats,
whole grains, legumes and some seafoods (oysters are very rich). White
bread, fats and sugar contain little or none (Murphy, *et al.*, 1975).
    Chromium is of recent importance as a nutrient. It was only shown to
be essential for rats as recently as 1959 (Schwarz and Mertz). The most
prominent feature of deficiency is impaired glucose tolerance. Impaired
glucose tolerance in children with kwashiorkor has improved dramatically
after a single oral dose of 250 μg (Gurson and Saner, 1971). There have
been reports that a proportion of adult diabetics have improved after
weeks of treatment. The intriguing aspect of chromium is that in animals
inorganic chromium has very low activity: what is needed is an organic

form called 'glucose tolerance factor' (GTF) (Hambidge, 1974). Brewer's yeast is the richest source of GTF; its exact structure has not yet been worked out but it is said to contain nicotinic acid, glycine, glutamic acid and cystine (Levander, 1975). Other good sources are black pepper, liver, beef, bread (including white) and, on a dry weight basis, mushrooms and beer.

Are any of the micronutrients likely to become more important with future changes in food supply and handling?
It is impossible to make more than a few guesses and suggest the sort of things we have to watch for. It is extremely difficult to make short-term estimates of the availability of food. Who could have guessed that potatoes would quadruple in price this year, sugar the year before and wheat the year before that? One trend I can discern is a continued decline of marine fish supplies unless there is a really big investment in fish farming. Fish are not important as a source of energy or protein but are the major natural source of iodine (Wayne, *et al.*, 1964). As sea fish supplies dwindle we shall have to give more attention to dietary iodine.

Some expect and some would like to see a reduction in our meat intake and its replacement by such products as textured vegetable protein. The Food Standards Committee (1974b) and Committee on Medical Aspects of Food Policy are watching the nutritional implications. But even if iron is put back into novel protein foods it is unlikely to be as well absorbed as haemoglobin or muscle iron (Martinez-Torres and Layrisse, 1971) and trace elements like zinc will probably have to be considered in more detail than they have been.

A change in food preservation which might have nutritional effects is a reduction in canning, using tin plated steel cans and their replacement by aluminium cans, plastic containers or freezing. This, along with the earlier replacement of iron cooking pots by aluminium is likely to reduce our iron intakes (Moore, 1973).

Deep freezing has a gentler effect than canning on the well known heat-labile nutrients like ascorbic acid and thiamin. However, losses of vitamin E are substantial during frozen storage (Bunnell, *et al.*, 1965). We do not seem to have information as yet about the effect of prolonged exposure of light-sensitive nutrients to light in cold display cabinets.

There are many other possible ways in which the intakes of individual micronutrients can become more or less critical in the future—from unexpected shortages, new cultivars, new methods of agriculture and animal husbandry, new processing, preservation and preparation methods, new antagonists, etc. Two things are certain: there will be changes in the micronutrients in our foods and some of these will take us by surprise.

When we know that a certain section of the population has a low intake of a micronutrient the appropriate measures will vary. Sometimes the susceptible group come under the auspices of clinical medicine—this is so with vitamin K, magnesium, sodium, chloride, potassium and EFA. The solution to these problems depends on good nutrition information throughout the medical profession.

For other nutrients, which come more in to public health, several very different strategies are possible—restoration or enrichment of foods (as with thiamin in bread), or medical surveillance (as is the British policy for iron deficiency), or education in nutrition and healthy habits (which is being used for vitamin D at present), or food subsidies. It is very important to choose the best course of action. Nearly all the micronutrients are inexpensive—except for biotin; they are often cheaper than most natural dietary sources (Lockie, 1972) and these prices may become even more in favour of the pure synthetic nutrients in the future. Already Friend (1973) has estimated that in the US food supply enrichment accounts for 40% of the thiamin, 25% of the iron, 20% of the niacin, 15% of the riboflavin and 10% of vitamins A and C. The US and the Swedish Nutrition Foundations have prepared some useful proposed guidelines for utilisation of industrially produced nutrients (Darby and Hambraeus, 1975) which I would recommend to those who have not seen them.

But as these guidelines make clear, food enrichment cannot be used for all nutritional problems and by deliberately not pressing ahead with increased iron enrichment of bread—a policy explained by Callender (1973a) at the last BNF Conference—we in Britain seem to have had less trouble with iron than the Americans have had (Crosby, 1975; Anon., 1975).

Working out the best measures to correct poor nutrition or prevent deficiency disease needs a lot of careful thought and full discussion round the problem. This country has an interesting and effective record of achievement in doing this and we have, I think, an effective structural organisation for the purpose. But applied nutrition measures cannot be applied until the problem has been found and there is no simple way of predicting where the next one will turn up in a complex society struggling to pay its way in a changing world. We need strong, innovative and diverse nutrition research in this country, as the Neuberger report (Agricultural Research Council/Medical Research Council, 1974) made clear.

REFERENCES

Adams, P. W., Wynn, V., Rose, D. P., Seed, M., Folkard, J. and Strong, R. (1973). *Lancet*, **1**, 897.
Agricultural Research Council/Medical Research Council (1974). *Food and Nutrition Research*, Report of the ARC/MRC committee, HMSO, London.
Al Rashid, R. A. and Spangler, J. (1971). *New Engl. J. Med.*, **285**, 841.

68	A. S. TRUSWELL

Anon. (1973). *Lancet*, **1**, 1097.
Anon. (1975). *Nutr. Rev.*, **33**, 46.
Arneil, G. C. and Crosbie, J. C. (1963). *Lancet*, **2**, 423.
Baron, J. H. and Oliver, L. C. (1958). *Lancet*, **1**, 354.
Beaven, G. H., Dixon, G. H. and White, J. C. (1966). *Br. J. Haemat.*, **12**, 777.
Bengoa, J. M. (1973). In *Man, Food and Nutrition*, p. 1. Edited by M. Rechcigl, Jr., CRC Press, Cleveland, Ohio.
Britt, R. P., Harper, C. and Spray, G. H. (1971). *Quart. J. Med.*, **40**, 499.
Brook, M. (1973). In *Nutritional Deficiencies in Modern Societies*, p. 45. Edited by A. N. Howard and I. McLean Baird, Newman Books Ltd, London.
Bunnell, R. H., Keating, J., Quaresimo, A. and Parman, G. K. (1965). *Am. J. clin. Nutr.*, **17**, 1.
Byrne-Quinn, E. and Fessas, C. (1969). *Br. med. J.*, **4**, 25.
Callender, S. (1973a). In *Nutritional Problems in a Changing World*, p. 205. Edited by D. Hollingsworth and M. Russell, Applied Science, London.
Callender, S. (1973b). In *Nutritional Deficiencies in Modern Society*, p. 8. Edited by A. N. Howard and I. McLean Baird, Newman Books Ltd, London.
Carney, M. W. P. (1971). *Br. med. J.*, **2**, 110.
Coelingh Bennink, H. J. T. and Schreurs, W. H. P. (1975). *Br. med. J.*, **3**, 13.
Collins, F. D., Sinclair, A. J., Royle, J. B., Coats, D. A., Maynard, A. T. and Leonard, F. L. (1971). *Nutr. Metab.*, **13**, 150.
Cordano, A., Baertle, J. M. and Graham, G. G. (1964). *Pediatrics*, **34**, 324.
Coursin, D. B. (1954). *J. Am. med. Ass.*, **154**, 406.
Crosby, W. H. (1975). *J. Am. med. Ass.*, **231**, 1054.
Darby, W. J. and Hambraeus, L. (1975). *Näringsforskning*, **19**, 113.
Davidson, S. and Passmore, R. (1969). *Human Nutrition and Dietetics*, 4th edition, E. and S. Livingstone, Edinburgh and London.
Department of Health and Social Security (1969). *Recommended Intakes of Nutrients for the United Kingdom*, Reports on Public Health and Medical Subjects, No. 120. HMSO, London.
Department of Health and Social Security (1972). *A Nutrition Survey of the Elderly*, Reports on Health and Social Subjects, No. 3, HMSO, London.
Deutsche Gesellschaft für Ernährung (1975). *Empfehlungen für die Nährstoffzufuhr*, Umschau Verlag, Frankfurt am Main.
Flink, E. B., Stutzman, F. L., Anderson, A., Konig, A. R. and Fraser, R. (1954). *J. Lab. clin. Med.*, **43**, 169.
Food Standards Committee (1974a). *Second Report on Bread and Flour*, HMSO, London.
Food Standards Committee (1974b). *Report on Novel Protein Foods*, HMSO, London.
Friend, B. (1973). *Enrichment and Fortification of Foods*, 1966–70, US Department of Agriculture, Agricultural Research Service, Consumer and Food Economics Institute, Hyattsville, Maryland 20782.
Giles, C. and Shuttleworth, E. M. (1958). *Lancet*, **2**, 1341.
Gurson, C. T. and Saner, G. (1971). *Am. J. clin. Nutr.*, **24**, 1313.
Hallberg, L. (1966). *Acta obst. Gynec. Scand.*, **45**, 25.
Hallberg, L. (1975). *Näringsforskning*, **19**, 4.

Halsted, J. A., Ronaghy, H. A., Abadi, P., Haghshenas, M., Amirhakemi, G. H., Barakat, R. M. and Reinhold, J. G. (1972). *Am. J. Med.*, **53**, 277.
Hambidge, K. M. (1974). *Am. J. clin. Nutr.*, **27**, 505.
Hambidge, K. M., Hambidge, M., Jacobs, M. and Baum, J. D. (1972). *Pediat. Res.*, **6**, 868.
Hanna, S., Harrison, M., MacIntyre, I. and Fraser, R. (1960). *Lancet*, **2**, 172.
Hansen, A. E., Adam, D. J. D., Boelsche, A. N., Haggard, M. E., Wiese, H. F., Pratt, E. L. and Hunter, V. (1957). *Fed. Proc.*, **16**, 387.
Hassan, H., Hashim, S. A., Van Itallie, T. B. and Sebrell, W. H. (1966). *Am. J. clin. Nutr.*, **19**, 147.
Hibbard, B. M. (1964). *J. Obstet. Gynaec. Br. Commonw.*, **71**, 529.
Hoffbrand, A. V. (1970). *Archs Dis. Childh.*, **45**, 441.
Hopkins, L. L., Jr., Ransome-Kuti, O. and Majaj, A. S. (1968). *Am. J. clin. Nutr.*, **21**, 203.
Ibbotson, R. M., Colvin, B. T. and Colvin, M. P. (1975). *Br. med. J.*, **4**, 145.
Kensler, C. J. and Langermann, H. (1954). *Proc. Soc. exp. Biol. Med.*, **85**, 364.
Levander, O. A. (1975). *J. Am. diet. Ass.*, **66**, 338.
Lockie, G. M. (1972). *Nutrition, Lond.*, **26**, 8.
Lotz, M., Zisman, E. and Bartter, F. C. (1968). *New Engl. J. Med.*, **278**, 409.
Martinez-Torres, C. and Layrisse, M. (1971). *Am. J. clin. Nutr.*, **25**, 531.
McIntyre, N. and Stanley, N. N. (1971). *Br. med. J.*, **3**, 567.
Milne, J. S., Lonergan, M. E., Williamson, J., Moore, F. M. L., McMaster, R. and Percy, N. (1971). *Br. med. J.*, **4**, 383.
Ministry of Agriculture, Fisheries and Food (1975). *Food Facts No.* 13, *September*, MAFF Press Office, London.
Moore, C. V. (1973). In *Modern Nutrition in Health and Disease—Dietotherapy*, 5th edition, p. 299. Edited by R. S. Goodhart and M. E. Shils, Lea and Febiger, Philadelphia.
Moynahan, E. J. (1974). *Lancet*, **2**, 399.
Murphy, E. W., Willis, B. W. and Watt, B. K. (1975). *J. Am. diet. Ass.*, **66**, 345.
Osborn-White, W. S. and Smith, R. M. (1973). *Biochem. J.*, **136**, 265.
Philip, G. and Smith, J. F. (1973). *Lancet*, **2**, 122.
Prasad, A. S., Miale, A., Farid, Z., Sandstead, H. H., Schulert, A. R. and Darby, W. J. (1963). *Archs intern. Med.*, **111**, 407.
Roberts, P. D., James, H., Petrie, A., Morgan, J. O. and Hoffbrand, A. V. (1973). *Br. med. J.*, **3**, 67.
Royal College of Physicians: Committee on the Fluoridation of Water Supplies (1976). *Fluoride, Teeth and Health*, Pitman Medical, London.
Schumacher, H. R., Bernhart, F. W. and Gyorgy, P. (1975). *Am. J. clin. Nutr.*, **28**, 1200.
Schwarz, K. and Mertz, W. (1959). *Archs Biochem. Biophys.*, **85**, 292.
Schwarz, K. and Milne, D. B. (1972). *Bio-inorganic Chem.*, **1**, 331.
Shane, B. and Contractor, S. F. (1975). *Am. J. clin. Nutr.*, **28**, 739.
Snyderman, S. E., Holt, L. E., Jr., Carretero, R. and Jacobs, K. G. (1953). *Am. J. clin. Nutr.*, **1**, 200.
Stewart, J. S., Roberts, P. D. and Hoffbrand, A. V. (1970). *Lancet*, **2**, 542.
Svejcar, J. and Homolka, J. (1950). *Ann. Paediat.*, **174**, 175.

Temperley, I. J., Meehan, M. J. M. and Gatenby, P. B. B. (1968). *Br. J. Haemat.*, **14**, 13.
Truswell, A. S. (1973). *Update*, **7**, 179.
Varadi, S., Abbot, D. and Elwis, A. (1966). *J. clin. Path.*, **19**, 33.
Wayne, E. J., Koutras, D. A. and Alexander, W. D. (1964). *Clinical Aspects of Iodine Metabolism*, Blackwell, Oxford.
West Derbyshire Medical Society (1966). *Lancet*, **2**, 959.
Wardrop, C. A. J., Heatley, R. V., Tennant, G. B. and Hughes, L. E. (1975). *Lancet*, **2**, 640.
Willoughby, M. L. N. (1967). *Br. J. Haemat.*, **13**, 503.
WHO (1972). *Nutrition: A Review of the WHO Programme 1965–1971*, WHO, Geneva.
Wretlind, A. (1975). *Bibl. Nutr. et Dieta.*, No. 21, p. 177, Karger, Basel.

CHAPTER 7

Future food and nutrition policy in Norway

N. EEG-LARSEN and M. EGGEN OGRIM

University of Oslo

On November 7, 1975 the Norwegian government presented a comprehensive report 'On Norwegian Nutrition and Food Policy' to the *Storting* (the Norwegian parliament). The report was worked out under the auspices of the ministries which are responsible for food supply (agriculture, fisheries and foreign trade), health, consumer affairs and education. The National Nutrition Council (*Statens Ernæringsråd*), which is also the national FAO committee, had two representatives in the group that prepared the report.

The report deals with a long term programme for the period 1975-1990. The summary starts with the following sentences:

'In the view of the government, the nutrition and food policy should coordinate several important objectives and considerations. These may be summarised as follows:

1. Healthy dietary habits should be encouraged.
2. A nutrition and food policy should be formulated in accordance with the recommendations of the World Food Conference.
3. For reasons connected with supply, the policy should aim at increased production and consumption of domestic food and at strengthening the ability to increase rapidly the degree of self sufficiency in the food supply.
4. For regional policy reasons, the highest priority should be placed on utilising the food production resources in the economically weaker areas.

One of the main tasks of the future nutrition and food policy will be the *active coordination* of these considerations.'

With such extensive objectives, the report had to deal with a diversity of subjects. Matters concerning nutrition and diet are handled in two ways in the report. They are discussed both from the point of view of the nutritionist and from a political angle. Dietary trends since the beginning of the century are described. During this period, the food supply in Norway as in other Western countries, has become more plentiful and varied. At the same time, the general economic standard and the standard of social security have improved and there has been a lessening of the differences between social classes. Especially since the First World War, the authorities have endeavoured in various ways to improve the quality of the diet. Examples of the measures used are school meals; dietary education at mother and child clinics, in schools and through other channels; and the use of legislation as a means of influencing the composition of important foods.

These changes have led to an improved diet with better supplies of several essential nutrients. Deficiency diseases such as scurvy and rickets have practically disappeared. There has been considerable improvement in the general state of health, as measured in terms of infant mortality, growth and development of children and adolescents, and resistance to infectious diseases. There is no doubt that better diet is one of the factors which has brought about these changes.

Along with this development there has, however, been an increase in some diseases related to diet, especially the cardiovascular diseases, which are now the most frequent cause of death. The particularly unfavourable aspect of these diseases is that they kill so many middle aged men and disable even more. While the life expectancy of the new born infant has been steadily increasing, the expected life span of men of 50 years of age has shown a decline in the period from 1960 to 1970.

The relationship between diet and cardiovascular diseases is not entirely understood. Most Norwegian nutritionists feel, however, that enough knowledge exists to warrant alterations in the diet with the aim of preventing cardiovascular diseases. Recommendations as to the amount and kind of fats in the diet were issued in 1975 by the National Nutrition Council. These are supplements to earlier recommendations concerning the intake of essential nutrients.

We will not enter into details about the figures selected, but will briefly discuss the way in which the recommendations are presented. This is especially important when the advice is supposed to form the basis of a nutrition and food supply policy.

A good diet has to satisfy two sets of criteria: it should be both *forsvarlig* and *hensiktsmessig*. The nearest translation to *forsvarlig* is safe. A safe diet is defined as a diet which, according to our present knowledge, permits general good health and is not known to have any detrimental effects. We find it important to discourage the use of words such as 'ideal', 'optimal' or 'correct' in connection with diet. We stress the fact that diet may permit but cannot guarantee good health. Theoretically a safe diet may be obtained through an infinite number of food combinations. To be *hensiktsmessig* (suitable, appropriate) the food combinations must be practical. This means first that they must be acceptable to the consumers. This implies, above all, that the foods and amounts suggested permit a meal pattern which is considered 'normal' by the majority of the population.

In planning a national food and nutrition policy, additional factors such as domestic food production and the state of the economy will weigh heavily in the judgement of what is considered suitable.

The nutritional part of the report concludes with an evaluation of our present diet and a summary of the focal points in the long term planning of the future national diet. These points are:

To secure enough food for the population. A sufficient supply is a prerequisite of safe nutrition. (It is necessary to stress this, as there has been so much talk about overeating and obesity that some people consider that foods' ability to provide energy as something undesirable);

To correct the weaknesses of our present diet, which implies a reduction of the proportion of fat in the diet and an increase in the share of polyunsaturated fatty acids in the total fat. The drop in energy from fat should be replaced by an increase in energy from starch;

To preserve the favourable aspects of our diet. The level of intake of most nutrients is at present considered satisfactory. The supply of iron, however, creates problems which are not entirely solved.

It is stressed that premature coronary heart diseases, dental caries and other diseases characteristic of affluent countries must be defeated by correcting diet as well as factors related to environment and behaviour. A safe diet is regarded as an important part of primary preventive health work. It is stated in the report that the government will endeavour to follow the experts' advice in the formulation of its nutritional policy.

Calculated on an energy basis, Norway imports about half the food going into human consumption. Increased self sufficiency is an important aim both from a national and from a global point of view. Accordingly, problems regarding domestic food production have a prominent place in the report.

During the last few decades, the agricultural area has gradually been reduced, and is now about 0·9 million hectares (Mha). In the government's view the aim should be to increase the cultivated area to 1 Mha in 1990. This should be obtained by restricting the use of productive land for development purposes, recultivation of areas lying idle and cultivation of new land. The area used for grain production should be increased from the present 0·3 Mha to 0·36 Mha by 1990.

A considerable proportion of the increase should be used for bread grain. More rough fodder should be produced in order to make a greater part of the imported and home produced grain available for human consumption. The increase in agricultural production envisaged will diverge in some ways from the line of development which has been followed in Norway in recent years. The decline in agricultural employment will have to be lessened and the gross investment in agriculture will have to be greater than previously calculated.

During the last 30 years, there has been a large increase in yield in agriculture and animal husbandry. This is due to extensive use of fertiliser, improved strains of crops and improved breeds of domestic animals, as well as to improved feeding methods and mechanisation. Continued and intensified agricultural research is considered to be a prerequisite for further increases in yield.

Fishing has traditionally been an important trade in Norway. Fish consumption is higher than in most other countries. A large part of the catch is, however, exported or used for production of animal fodder and marine oils. Fishing and fishing industries are of considerable economic value, and are, among other things, important for the stabilisation of the population in many economically weaker areas. The fishing grounds in the North East Atlantic are some of the most exploited in the world. As pointed out in the report, it is of primary importance to obtain international agreements which regulate the catches and prevent overexploitation of spawning and young fish. It is considered desirable that the greater part of the fish landed should be used for human consumption. Measures to achieve this (e.g. improved utilisation and development of new fish-based products) are discussed. The need for an increase in research into various fishery problems is pointed out. It is, among other things, important to concentrate on the resources which form the primary base of Norwegian fisheries and to locate and chart possible new ones.

The report discusses the possibilities of increasing the food supply from other traditional Norwegian sources, such as whaling and sealing, hunting, inland fishing, gathering of wild berries.

The importance of finding ways of using the various foodstuffs as effectively as possible and of minimising waste at all stages of processing, distribution and handling of food is emphasised.

In order to moderate the adverse effects of variations in production yields and temporary international trade difficulties, plans are worked out to extend the emergency stocks of cereals. Long term food trade arrangements, especially with neighbouring countries, are also of primary importance. Table 1 shows the average food consumption in 1974 (based on statistics at the wholesale level) and the proposed consumption in 1990 may be taken as a summary of the government's aims for the development of the consumption pattern.

The main nutritional difference between our present diet and the aims for 1990 is that the part of the energy derived from fat is lowered from about 42% to about 35%. The fatty acid composition of the diet is largely dependent on the composition of the margarine. The differences in content of most essential nutrients are small. The contents of vitamins A and D in the diet largely depend on the level of fortification of margarine. A considerable rise in the consumption of cereal grain is expected. This is an inescapable consequence of a reduction in the fat content of the diet. A decrease in the fat consumption may be achieved in various ways. The main sources of fats in our national diet are margarine and other fats

TABLE 1

NORWEGIAN FOOD SUPPLIES AT THE
WHOLESALE LEVEL

(kg per head per year)

	1974	1990
Cereals (flour)	72	90
Potatoes	83	90
Vegetables	39	42
Fruit	70	76
Meat	48	48
Fish	28	40
Eggs	10	10
Milk, whole	172	135
Milk, skim	19	60
Cheese	10	10
Butter	5	6·5
Margarine	19	13
Other fats (edible oils, etc.)	6	4
Sugar[a]	30	35

[a] There was a steep rise in the price of sugar in Norway in 1974 and a drop in recorded consumption at the wholesale level. To what degree this reflects a decrease in actual intake is still unknown. The proposed consumption in 1990 is somewhat lower than the figures for the years 1970–1973.

(43% of the total supply), milk and milk products including butter (33%) and meat (17%).

Cutting down the consumption of any of these food commodities will have both primary and secondary economic effects. In the solution suggested by the government, the main part of the reduction is achieved by a decrease in margarine consumption.

It must be pointed out that milk and meat production is the backbone of Norwegian agriculture. It is necessary for the stabilisation of population resettlement in many economically weaker areas, because grazing land in the mountains and the northern parts of the country can be utilised by ruminants. Meat consumption has increased considerably in recent years and it is considered desirable to limit this development.

About half of the fat used in margarine is derived from hydrogenated marine fat. The production of this is closely connected with the production of fish meal for fodder. In the view of the government a decrease in total consumption of margarine would make it possible to substitute part of the imported hydrogenated vegetable fat with hydrogenated marine oils. The intake of marine fat *per caput* could thus remain as at present.

The changes in diet must be made voluntarily and in the individual households. The government can, however, influence the development through various political measures. During the postwar years, price subsidies of foods have been extensively used as a means of controlling the general price level. A special objective has been to benefit families with small children and other low income consumers. Nutritional considerations have had limited influence. In the government's view, considerations of price must still be an important base for its policy of subsidies. The government is, however, of the opinion that it will be possible to combine this with the aim of influencing the consumption of food in a direction which is desirable from a nutritional point of view.

It is considered essential to extend and improve the teaching of nutrition in various educational establishments. The teaching should provide motivation for better dietary habits and supply knowledge about nutritional principles and about food composition. Training in proper planning and preparation of meals is considered to be an important part of dietary education. The importance of good basic training and possibilities for the further education of teachers are pointed out. The situation regarding textbooks and teaching aids needs to be improved. Knowledge concerning nutrition and diet should have a broader place in the curriculum at medical schools as well as in the education of other groups who have the responsibility for giving advice on health matters.

The government proposes a campaign with the aim of improving the dietary habits of the population. Much of the work may be carried out by the great voluntary organisations, many of which have long traditions in advisory work. A prerequisite for good results is that the activities should be coordinated and that sound and appropriate information material, suitable for various groups and purposes, is supplied.

An important way of influencing the nutrition of the population is through regulating the composition of basic foods. During the last 25 years margarine has been compulsorily fortified with vitamins A and D, and the minimum extraction rate for wheat flour has been 78%. These are examples of legislative measures which have considerable impact on the intake of some nutrients.

The measures which the government intend to use to further the aims which have been outlined can be divided into the following groups:

consumer subsidies; agricultural and fishery policies; improved methods of industrial processing; distribution and marketing; legislation and regulatory provisions; research; education and information. The importance of an integrated approach is pointed out.

The report finally sketches the framework of new governmental bodies with special responsibility for future nutrition and food policies; it plans for a reorganisation of the National Nutrition Council. The actual planning will have to await the debate on the report in the *Storting*, which is scheduled to take place in May 1976. (The main part of the report is to be translated into English.)

CHAPTER 8

The People's Republic of China: agriculture and food provision

K. L. BLAXTER

Rowett Research Institute, Aberdeen

Current developments in the People's Republic of China are of considerable interest in relation to the problem implicit in the title of this Conference, namely the relationship between Food and People. These developments do in fact suggest that in one country at any rate, the seemingly intractable problem of providing a sufficient supply of safe, nutritionally adequate food for a massive population for long at a subsistence level, is not only capable of solution but can be solved. Whether the solution is a stable one, whether it is separable from the political framework of ideas in which it has taken place cannot be stated; all that I wish and can do is to give my impression of the Republic and attempt an analysis.

I am not, of course, a sinologist. My knowledge of China stems from a visit I made to the Republic last summer as a member of a delegation of the Royal Society led by Professor J. Harley of Oxford, which was specifically invited by the Academica Sinica to see the agricultural development and research being undertaken in the country. Such was the fascination of the Republic that since my return I have obtained much additional information from both official Chinese and other sources about various facets of their economy.

It is essential at the outset to realise the size of China and thus obtain a perspective. The country is immense. The land area is double that of Europe and of the same order as that of the United States of America. Its population, currently estimated at 840 million people, is greater than the population of the Soviet Union and the United States of America put together. The population of China, including the autonomous regions, in fact exceeds considerably that of what FAO calls the developed world, and the Chinese in conversation clearly identify with the developing countries of the world, which they clearly dominate. In addition, they account for more than two thirds of all those people who live in the centrally planned economies of the world, that is the Communist countries.

Statistics of this comparative sort do not illustrate China's problem. The land resource is limited. West of a line running from the Great Kingan in Mongolia, through the north east elbow of the Yellow River to

the mountains of Tibet and Yunnan, agriculture is limited by lack of
rainfall and poverty of soil to oasis farming, indeed much of the area of
Sinkiang is unpopulated. Agriculture is confined to the north and south
China plains, with some taking place in the arid North West, Manchuria,
the loess uplands and on the uplands of the Yung Kuei plateau. Though
there are 960 million hectares of total land, 40 times more than in the
United Kingdom, the agricultural land is only 127 million hectares, a
mere 18 times that in the United Kingdom. The problem is one of limited
land for many people, 840 millions on 127 million hectares! The population
of China is about 15 times our own. The amount of cropped land in China
is currently 0·15 ha/person compared with 0·13 ha/person in the United
Kingdom; they have slightly more land than we do. We, however, meet
only about 47% of our food energy needs. China meets its whole requirement and, in addition, provides much basic food for Hong Kong and
Macao. The current harvest of grain announced earlier this year, namely
290 million tons, is an adequate supply for her people, and China has not
entered world markets for the purchase of grain for many years.

To understand what has been achieved it is essential to appreciate
something of the recent agricultural history of the country and, more
specifically, the remarkable fact that the achievement has been accomplished
through the exercise of a political ideology based on Marxism–Leninism
as interpreted by the Chairman of the Communist Party of China, Mao
Tsetung. The history is characterised by changes of course and in particular
by a rejection of the Soviet pattern of Communism, a pattern now reviled
by the Chinese under the name revisionism. Present agrarian structures
are the result of a series of changes undertaken within a framework of
political ideas.

When the Kuomintang was defeated in 1949, the People's Republic
was declared and the first step to be taken was a redistribution of land
coupled with a repudiation of all contractual agreements relating to land.
In addition, and no doubt under Russian influence, a number of state
farms were established at that time; few of these remain and are not
further considered. In the redistribution of land each family was on average
allocated about one hectare, more in the North, less in the South. The land
was owned by the family, but every encouragement was given to the
formation of cooperatives, such that by 1954 about 60% of all farms took
part in some form of cooperation.

Little or no rationalisation of field size took place at this time and
slowly and inexorably all the older features of the social system before
land reform emerged—selling of one's own labour, dealing in land and
borrowing on land security. Mao himself at this time (July 1955) wrote:
'The spontaneous forces of capitalism have been steadily growing in the
countryside in recent years, with new rich peasants springing up everywhere and many well to-do middle peasants striving to become rich

peasants. On the other hand, many poor peasants are still living in poverty for lack of sufficient means of production with some in debt and others selling or renting out their land.'

The Communist Party regarded this as understandable but intolerable, quoting Lenin 'small production engenders capitalism and the bourgeoisie, continuously, daily, hourly, spontaneously and on a massive scale'.

The first five year plan of 1953–1957 was on the Russian model, emphasising heavy industrial investment with only 6% of the total investment being made in agriculture. Before its completion, however, in December 1955, collectivisation was imposed, that is the transfer of land to cooperative ownership. The collectivisation involved formation of production teams of 200 or more families and their resources, and a change in accounting from the family to this higher level. This was undoubtedly the most important single step taken by the Chinese for it enabled a rationalisation of farming, notably of field size, to take place, and provided the massive labour force for manual tasks such as terracing, making new land, flood control, reservoir and well construction. The whole process was completed within a year; by December 1956 88% of all families were within Production Brigades. Some private lands—about 50 m²—were retained by the individual family for home production of food.

A divergence from the Soviet pattern was already discernible when Mao published in 1957 his analysis of the social and political problems of China in a work entitled *On the correct handling of contradictions among the people*. This stated that the investment policy had not hitherto been correct and a much quoted part reads: 'In discussing our path to industrialisation I am here concerned principally with the relation between the growth of heavy industry, light industry and agriculture. It must be affirmed that heavy industry is the core of China's economic construction. At the same time, full attention must be paid to the development of light industry. . . . As China is a large agricultural country with over 80% of her population in the rural areas, industry must develop together with agriculture, for only thus can industry secure raw materials and a market, and only thus is it possible to accumulate fairly large funds for building a powerful heavy industry.' This approach states that wealth can only arise from an agricultural base; there are no short cuts, and this basic attitude has dominated economic thought in China ever since.

The following year, in 1958, the *Great Leap Forward* was announced. This consisted of the next step, the establishment of the communes, that is a collective grouping of the Production Brigades. The object was to force the pace of the revolution to achieve self sufficiency in food and extend village industrialisation. The final structure in the Republic was 74 000 communes each with an average of 7 brigades and 40 production teams. A commune had an area of about 4000 hectares to support 4000–5000 families.

The *Great Leap Forward* was probably instituted prematurely, possibly as a result of the ideological struggle in the communist world as between Mao and Kruschev. Certainly, there were serious administrative problems in its implementation exacerbated when the Russians withdrew all aid and technical help in 1960. It was particularly unfortunate that agriculturally disastrous weather for three successive years followed the establishment of the communes. Liu Shao Chi, a capable administrator, rose to power as Chairman of the Central People's Government at this time and what followed was an attempt at central direction of the communes. This gave rise to an intellectual elite, advising the peasants what to do. Just as he had done some 10 years previously, Mao apparently realised that the fundamental principles he professed were being eroded, and the Great Proletarian Cultural Revolution followed. This was basically a struggle between Mao Tsetung's ideology and the pragmatic approach of Liu Shao Chi, in which emphasis was given to production at all costs and which led to the revival of old differences—between town and country folk, between those who worked with their hands and those with their minds and between industry and agriculture. Basically Mao wished to prevent a drift towards revisionism of the Soviet pattern. It is of interest that although Lin Piao had edited the Little Red Book (the Thoughts of Chairman Mao) and was clearly involved in the Cultural Revolution, he is now denigrated in China and his name is linked with those of Confucius and Mencius in terms which suggest his name is becoming synonymous with elitism. The current campaign against former vice premier Teng, who was out of favour for many years following the Cultural Revolution, is also couched in terms of revisionism. Clearly the new Maoism is firmly associated with prevention of the emergence of any elitist element, and is in accord with the precept of continuing revolution.

The current structures in agriculture are the result of these political struggles and changes. The basic unit is the production brigade, made up of production teams. The brigades make up the communes which are the rural power centres combining governmental administration and the technical and financial management of the commune itself. A county is the next highest unit, and there are 2200 of these in the Republic. There are signs that a new emphasis on the county as an agricultural industrial unit is likely soon to emerge as judged by conferences recently held to make 'Tachai-type counties', that is counties which emulate the most progressive of the brigades. The next highest unit is the province which may be divided into prefectures. Political direction is exercised by the Party and by Revolutionary Councils elected by Local People's Congresses. At every level there are Revolutionary Committees which are concerned with a strengthening of political rather than managerial direction of every cooperative aspect of life.

At the Brigade level the individual elects to accomplish certain tasks for a certain number of 'work points'. The income of the whole brigade consists of that from the sale of one tenth of their produce to the State at a fixed high price, the grain they need for feeding themselves together with the money obtained by selling produce on the free fixed price market. The brigade decides collectively what it wishes to invest in terms of new machinery, capital goods and how much it wishes to distribute. The individual receives remuneration in proportion to his contribution.

Fig. 1.   Terracing at Tachai production brigade.

Consumer goods are available to him or he can invest his money at interest. The system is thus a decentralised agrarian communism but differs from the classical Marxist view 'From each according to his ability, to each according to his needs'.

It will be evident that political belief is the main determinant of agrarian structures, and that the incredible singleness of mind of that remarkable man Mao Tsetung has largely been responsible for the present emphasis on the central importance of food production.

Food, however, must be related to people. The Chinese have not been slow to adopt the classical Marxist attitude to population. Marx (*Das Kapital*) is quoted: 'Capitalistic accumulation itself constantly produces a relatively redundant population of labourers, *i.e.* a population of greater extent than suffices for the average needs of the self-expansion of capital, and therefore a surplus population.' Similarly, the Chinese criticise Malthus, particularly his example of China written nearly 200 years ago in which he thought China could hardly double its produce in any number of years. They point out that although her population has increased by 60% in the last 25 years, China's grain output has increased 2·4 fold. These arguments, however, are hardly relevant; Marx referred to the unemployed, while Malthus was concerned with the forces maintaining a balance between the numbers of people and their means of subsistence rather than with statistical facts. As with agriculture, there have been changes of course within the Republic as far as population policy is concerned. A few years ago, population control was regarded as irrelevant, as exemplified by the slogan 'One more mouth to feed but two more hands to work.' Now there appear to be considerable social constraints on reproduction, which strangely emulate Malthus' third factor of moral restraint, together with direct approaches such as birth control practices, and pregnancy termination services. Marriage is late—about 27 years for men and 25 for women, and the family size norm is two. Birth control, using a pill of their own manufacture, is as far as I could ascertain practised by 70–80% of all women. Abortion by vacuum curettage is available in commune hospitals, apparently on demand, and I saw work being taken to the field scale on the use of prostaglandins for early termination of pregnancy. I asked about the rumour in the West that amniocentesis was being employed to determine sex, and that abortion was preferentially given to women carrying a female foetus, to find no knowledge about it on the part of those most likely to know. Certainly they have departed from the earlier Soviet pattern of medals for prolific motherhood, and are giving far more emphasis to sex equality. From the statistical information I have been able to gather it appears that the rate of natural increase of the population is now less than 1%, of the same order as that in the West and considerably less than that found in the developing countries of Africa and Latin America.

Nutritional status is apparently not monitored continuously, but data on birth weights of full-term babies show them to have increased since 1949. The Chinese do not exhibit the increase in stature which has been a characteristic feature of the Japanese in the last few decades, but it was my impression that visiting Chinese from Hong Kong were taller than the native Chinese. Certainly I saw no malnutrition; people looked very fit and had a great capacity for hard physical work, which they necessarily have to undertake.

The achievement of adequate nutritional status has been due to impressive advances in agricultural technology at the level of the production brigades. Technically, this has consisted of the improvement of land, the formation of new land, control of pests and diseases of crops, the breeding and dissemination of new crop varieties and the encouragement of multiple cropping, Control of flood water and the harnessing of water for irrigation has involved enormous tasks of civil engineering, while newer developments are towards mechanisation of labour-demanding tasks and an increase in animal production for food rather than for motive power and manure. The technical advances are largely based on traditional Chinese farming. What is new since the Cultural Revolution is the massive

Fig. 2.   Mountain scenery at Kuei-Lin in the autonomous region of Kwangsi Chuan.

harnessing of scientific manpower to achieve development. The scientific manpower trained in agriculture works directly with the peasants at the brigade level, returning to universities, colleges and research centres for refresher courses. There is no intermediate development agency, and it is stated that there are at least 10 million scientists working on agricultural problems in the Republic as a whole. The educated youth moved into the countryside during the Cultural Revolution to work with the peasants and this movement continues. Education is geared to these immediate practical ends, and involves direct participation by student and lecturer in day to day work in factories or on the land. The principle throughout is that scientists, peasants and revolutionary cadres work together.

All the evidence that is available suggests that the People's Republic of

China has accomplished more than most of those impoverished developing countries which caused concern to the world 25 years ago. She has increased the capital wealth of the whole country without massive unemployment or poverty of any sector, without creating a division between the rural and urban sectors of society and without massive growth of her cities and the appearance of any alienated minority. The supply of consumer goods is reasonable and is increasing and the people have pride in what they have achieved with their own hands. Furthermore, there is no evidence whatever that this has been achieved by methods which involve the punishment of recalcitrants, or the darker aspects of man's inhumanity to man. Those who fail or who 'take the capitalist road' are re-educated through criticism leading to self criticism. The people believe in what they are doing and subscribe to the central ethic of Marxism–Maoism.

There is much to admire, but equally room for concern. In agriculture there did not appear to me to be sufficient emphasis on the basic investigational work on which future development in farming must reside. No postgraduate education takes place, possibly because of the fear of creating a new intellectual elite, or a meritocracy. Again one wonders whether the extent of mechanisation of farming can be controlled, such that it stops at that point which yields no additional resource of land released from its role as a feed source for draft animals, and yields no benefit in increased industrial productivity through released manpower. That point in time may be far off since mechanisation will for many years be a boon, removing the sheer drudgery of hard physical work from the peasant and those who help him.

Finally, China's example may well provide hope to many peoples. The Chinese experiment shows that a population can learn to be self reliant and feed itself. That this has come about through a subscription to a particular social belief need not deter; where there is no horizon higher than an individual's own selfish need there is, to my mind, no hope.

PART 3

THE PROVISION OF FOOD

CHAPTER 9

Scientific progress in world food production

H. C. PEREIRA

Ministry of Agriculture, Fisheries and Food

Since the World Food Conference of November 1974 there have been so many studies, analyses and commentaries that I need not, for this audience, repeat the data and graphs. I will summarise only the conclusions from them on which there appears to be general agreement, and shall then outline the contribution which science is making to the increase of world food production.

The conclusions on which there appears to be a consensus are:

1. That although the total of world food supplies is still growing at about the same rate as the total world population the reserves in storage have fallen to a level which would be inadequate to meet another coincidence of poor crop seasons in major producing areas such as occurred in 1972–1973.
2. The geographical and economic discrepancies are increasing; USA, Australia, Canada and New Zealand have populations whose growth rates are slowing towards a position of stability, while their food production continues to rise. The USA alone has produced more than half of the world's food surplus of cereals and oilseeds available for export for the past 5 years and the estimates for this year suggest a yet higher proportion.
3. Europe's population growth is also slowing while agricultural production is increasing, so that the food imports are beginning to decline, although they still make a significant demand on world grain production.
4. The centrally directed economies of USSR and China, controlling about one third of the world's population, have been making increasing purchases from the declining food surplus of the rest of the world.
5. Africa, Asia and Latin America form the core of the world's food problem, with half of the world's population and more than three quarters of its growth increment massively dependent on primitive subsistence agriculture under the unstable regime of the inter-tropical

89

convergence zone. Although their food production has increased almost as much as that of the developed countries in the past 15 years, their population growth has cancelled out this advantage and has given no effective increase in the production *per caput*. As a result these countries are still unable to meet the crop failures which are an inescapable result of the variability in this great central belt of the world's atmospheric circulation system.

Among the major economic studies there is also a consensus that the primary solution to these problems must lie in improving the balance between food production and population needs in the developing countries themselves. The need is also recognised to improve the organisation of the more affluent international community to maintain reserves and to mobilise emergency aid to meet the disasters of drought and flood which will continue to occur. The problems of Asia, Africa and Latin America will not be solved by increasing transfer of food grains from North America. There is already evidence that this disrupts and discourages their home production and diverts political attention from the need to give overriding priority to the improvement of agriculture.

This matter of attaining a genuine and effective national priority for agriculture lies at the root of the problem of the developing countries. Priority for the application of science is here critical and as I shall illustrate later it can be highly effective, but in the tropical latitudes social prejudices have hindered the application of science to agriculture, which remains, for Asia, Africa and Latin America predominantly an occupation for the poor and ignorant, and one from which education is seen as a means of escape. In the higher latitudes science is far from being free from such social prejudices and emotional attitudes have impeded the application of research to the population problem.

The agricultural history of Europe clearly illustrates the problem which still faces the developing countries. For 1000 years agriculture suffered neglect which in Britain is very well documented. Two keen agricultural observers who were able and descriptive writers have defined this neglect. Virgil, in the Georgics, described in detail the agricultural techniques which the Romans brought to Britain and established over the first four centuries of the Christian era. In 1563 Fitzherbert's *Boke of Husbandry* gave a very explicit description of British agricultural practices, which are changed only in one important detail from those given by Virgil. This was to strengthen the wooden mouldboard of the plough by an iron tip, the ploughshare. Another 200 years elapsed before the British yeoman farmer, Jethro Tull, made the first major change in the system, not only by inventing both the seed-drill and the horse-hoe, but by growing his crops so successfully that Britain, and indeed the whole of Europe, rapidly adopted his methods. As agriculture became a recognised source of wealth, it also became an acceptable occupation for the able and ambitious, and thus it achieved the first essential stage of evolution into a modern industry. The second essential stage in progress was blocked by the industrial revolution. As a result of Britain's development of an economy based on export of manufactured goods in exchange for imports of farm produce, British agricultural production did not achieve the second essential stage of progress, which I would define as a national determination to increase our home-grown food supplies, until two successive world wars in 30 years had reminded us forcibly that we live on an island which can be blockaded. From 1950 onwards the combined agriculture and food industries began to develop the potential offered by our climate, soils and skills and to play their present major role in our national economy. Progress then depended on the third essential element, *i.e.* upon that combination of original research, innovative development and enterprising application which makes modern British agriculture a challenging and exciting pursuit.

The results were highly rewarding. Over the past two decades, 1950–1970, the yield of our crops and livestock rose in a manner which, if extended on a world scale, would already have solved the problems of world food supply. This growth in output was not achieved by expanding the farming areas; indeed, we have been losing some 60 000 acres of good land a year to road and building developments. Improvements in output were achieved by increased yields of crops and livestock. These increases stem directly from scientific research, interpreted through development stages into farming practice. The advances were adopted promptly by leading farmers and carried by an increasingly expert advisory service to the main body of the farming population. Agriculture is so complex an industry that advances in five main thrusts of research and development have to succeed simultaneously to bring these increases in yields about. All these scientific advances depend, for their application, on critically important support from the supply and service industries, so that cities now contribute materially to the agricultural production of a countryside. I will briefly describe the independent advances because the world's food supply will remain in jeopardy until these same advances have also been achieved in the tropical lands.

APPLICATION OF SCIENTIFIC KNOWLEDGE TO AGRICULTURAL PROBLEMS IN INDUSTRIALISED COUNTRIES

Nutrition

The first and most important increases were due to better nutrition for both crops and livestock. Crop nutrient requirements were approximately and often incompletely provided by the soil until 1840, when Liebig addressed the British Association and advanced a scientific basis for plant nutrition. Since then science, economics and field husbandry have together evolved a delicate balance by which the optimum dressings of nutrients are now supplied both as fertilisers and as organic manures.

This has permitted a substantial increase in plant populations so that well-nourished root systems add many tons of organic matter to the soil at each harvest. Research on the nutrition requirements of animals has similarly resulted in great improvements in growth rates and better conversion rates of foodstuffs into meat and milk. We have, however, particularly in Britain, made the mistake of specialising in crop and animal husbandry too independently, so that we are now having to put vigorous research and development into bulk handling of animal wastes to get them back onto the land.

Plant and animal breeding
While agriculture remains primitive, plants and animals are selected by survival at low planes of nutrition, while rarely capable of making profitable use of a more ample supply of nutrients. The breeding of improved varieties of crops and of strains of livestock capable of responding to better nutrition by more rapid growth rates and greater yields, provided the second main line of advance. Crop research has subsequently reached a further stage of producing strains capable of such rapid growth that they make better use of the nutrients available, even without fertilisers.

Crop and livestock protection from pests and diseases
The third main contribution by research and development was to the control of pests and diseases in both plants and animals. This is essentially a scientific battle which must begin by accurate studies of the life histories of the organisms which parasitise plants and animals and of the pests which attack them. Next the study of the delicate biochemical functioning of the enemy bodies permits the fashioning of chemicals which will attack the pest or pathogen without harming the host. This has become a major industry in which heavy investment both in scientific research and in manufacturing plant have been contributed by commercial enterprises. Insects and fungi have, however, shown rather alarming abilities to adapt to chemical attack by producing resistant strains. For this reason as well as those of high costs and the dangers of pollution there has been much determined research aimed at devising chemical agents which will attack only the pests and will spare their natural predators; thus biological control can be reinforced by chemical control. But for this we must tolerate some pest attacks. While both environmentalists and many practical agriculturalists favour biological control, the increasingly high standard of presentation, especially of fruit and vegetables, penalises any sign of damage. Thus even the low level of pests necessary to maintain the predators and to preserve the biological balance incurs heavy penalties in

the market. The most effective method of biological control is to seek strains of plants or of animals which are resistant to the attacks of pests and diseases. Throughout the world this is becoming one of the most important applications of science to agriculture.

Control of weeds

The fourth main scientific advance has been in weed control, again by a powerful combination of public and private research and manufacturing investment. Here the scientists have advanced beyond the devising of merely toxic chemicals to destroy weeds. They have achieved the simulation of plant hormones so that false growth instructions may be given to weed species, causing them to cooperate to their own destruction. To those of my generation who can recall the colourful weed infestations of prewar crops and pastures, today's tidy and business-like fields are a remarkable demonstration of agricultural progress. The long lines of field labourers hand-hoeing roots have been replaced by one man on a fast moving tractor spraying 6–8 acres/hour.

Application of power

This illustrates the fifth development which is the application of greatly increased power to farming operations. The techniques have sprung mainly from industrial research and development with valuable help from the agricultural engineering laboratories. They have resulted in a striking increase in power supply from one horse per full time worker at the end of the First World War to one tractor per man by 1965. The power of the tractors has increased from an average of 35 horsepower in 1950 to 52 horsepower in 1970.

The recent major increases in world oil prices direct attention to the great increase in total energy supply to British agriculture. While tractors in the fields are the most visible evidence, they consume only one seventh of the fuel input. The rest goes almost equally to fertilisers and to drying and storage of crops.

These five main advances, all independently necessary, have been achieved simultaneously in Britain over the two decades 1950–1970, with the result that a 40% increase in total output has been achieved, to reach a total value of some £4000 million per annum. The increased output has come from a slightly declining area of farmland and a rapidly decreasing labour force. Output per man has doubled over two decades. Although we are an industrial nation, our agricultural output is now greater than that of our iron and steel industry. Table 1 illustrates the yield increases in three major crops.

A year ago the government published a White Paper which gave a reasoned economic case for continuing to increase our food production at the rate of $2\frac{1}{2}$% a year. We still import half of our own food, much of which we could not grow in our temperate climate, but we also import 30% of the types of food which we are able to produce. This is partly for economic reasons but mainly because we could not grow on our own acres, food to satisfy our present diet. We could indeed produce a diet equal to, or better than, that which sustained us in the last war.

TABLE 1

IMPROVEMENT IN YIELDS OF BRITISH CROPS

(Average yields in England and Wales in tons/acre)

	1945	1955	1965	1975
Wheat	0·95	1·13	1·62	1·97
Barley	0·95	1·12	1·46	1·63
Potatoes	7·2	7·9	9·2	12·6

Sources: Ministry of Agriculture, Fisheries and Food (1968).
Ministry of Agriculture, Fisheries and Food, *Annual Reviews of Agriculture*.

We have, therefore, in these crowded islands, experienced the change from a neglected agriculture to one of high productivity. It is this change which the countries of Asia, Africa and Latin America must now bring about in the desperately short time enforced by the growth rates of their populations. It is therefore urgent that the full power of international science should be applied without delay to the problems of increasing the productivity of tropical agriculture.

THE INTERNATIONAL CENTRES FOR AGRICULTURAL RESEARCH

The great Foundations of the USA recognised this need and the Rockefeller Foundation pioneered in Mexico in 1943 a combined effort of crop improvement and agronomy development which changed that country from an economy whose major import was food to one in which the major export became wheat. As this enterprise in the objective application of science grew, the Ford Foundation and the USA Agency for International Development (AID) Organisation joined in. The success was so encouraging in wheat that a new joint effort was launched for rice, which is the staple food of one third of mankind. In 1960 the International Rice Research Institute (IRRI) was set up in the Philippines. In 1964 the joint effort in Mexico was expanded to form the International Centre for Improvement of Wheat and Maize, known by its Spanish acronym as CIMMYT. Both CIMMYT and IRRI have already made a substantial impact on the progress of tropical agriculture. The dwarf wheats from CIMMYT, highlighted by the well deserved award of a Nobel Prize to Norman Borlaug, and the fast growing rices from IRRI have been both used directly and also adapted to local conditions by plant breeders of national research services. The two Institutes were estimated in a recent study (Dalrymple, 1975) to have increased the value of the 1972/73 wheat and rice crop in Asia by over $1000 million in a year in which world production was below average. The successes have led to the remarkably rapid establishment of a unique association of donors, supporting a chain of International Centres girdling the tropical world (Fig. 1).

The consultative group and the technical advisory committee
Under the leadership of Robert McNamara, President of the World Bank, a meeting of donors was convened in 1971. A consortium was organised under the title of 'The Consultative Group for International Agricultural Research' (CGIAR). It began with 15 members among which was the UK Government and it has already grown to a membership of 22. In 1972 the total contributions amounted to $15 million and this year the total is likely to exceed $60 million. The World Bank provides a small administrative secretariat. The Consultative Group was set up in 1972, a Technical Advisory Committee (TAC) of 12 members, plus a Chairman, Sir John Crawford, the Australian agricultural economist, who is also Chancellor of the Australian National University at Canberra. Of the 12 members of the TAC, 10 are agricultural scientists and two are economists. At present six international centres are already built and in operation, while three more are under construction. The dynamic nature of this movement is such that the assembly of world collections of planting material and the setting up of screening trials, together with training courses for staff from developing countries begins in each case while the blueprint from the main capital development is being worked out. The International Board for Plant Genetic Resources is an additional enterprise and the Consultative Group is also contributing to a regional organisation of West African states to improve their production of rice.

The international centres maintain a very active exchange with their colleagues in the national research services in the countries which they are supporting. Plant breeders and agronomists from many developing countries spend a year or two gaining experience at the centres of modern methods of crop improvements, while outposted staff from the centres help in each region in which their crops are being grown. All of the major food crops of the tropical world are now being worked on.

CIMMYT (International Centre for Improvement of Wheat and Maize)
The main centre is about 20 miles from Mexico City and here many thousands of cross pollinations are made annually. The unique feature of

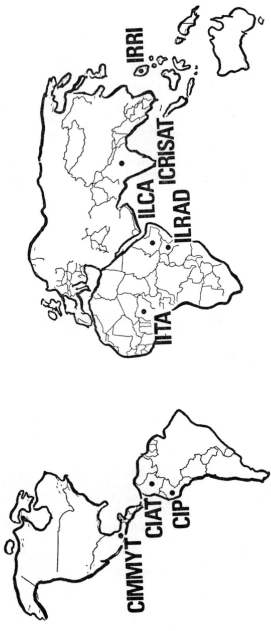

Fig. 1. The international centres. The centres already cover a wide range of tropical conditions.

the testing is the chain of substations, from hot conditions at sea level to the cold, wet conditions of an 8000 ft mountain station. Only varieties which yield well and show satisfactory disease resistance under this extreme range of conditions are retained for further testing. Wheats which pass these tests have proved remarkably adaptable. They go to over 1000 trial stations in 66 countries throughout the world. Maize varieties are tested at nearly 300 trial sites in 48 countries.

The centre also has a large programme on Triticale, the new cereal bred from crosses between wheat and rye. It has more protein of better quality than wheat and has much of the hardiness of rye. At present it is being tried out in 40 countries. Yields of over 6 t/ha have already been obtained. CIMMYT has also done valuable work on barley, but this will in due course be continued by a new centre which is being set up in the Middle East.

IRRI (International Rice Research Institute)

Improvements in the rice crop came rapidly from IRRI, with impressive increases in yield and in rate of growth. They bred and selected for short stiff-strawed varieties which could carry heavy yields without lodging. As with the CIMMYT wheats, the lines were selected to respond to fertiliser, but here it is essential to point out a serious error which has occurred in much of the public discussion of the new varieties. The new strains do indeed have the potential ability to respond to fertilisers, but without fertilisers they still do better than the traditional varieties. Their rapid growth makes the best use of available water and nutrients (Fig. 2). It is because they grow very much faster, and are less penalised by a sudden end to the rainy season (or a cut-off in irrigation) which is so characteristic a problem of the variable monsoons. Farmers now get two crops of rice a year and often have the third planted within 12 months. This has the advantage of keeping the crop within the local handling facilities, such as bullock carts. It has the very big disadvantage, however, of needing continuous human effort with the new crop to be planted as soon as the harvest is finished. This contrasts strongly with a long tradition of a season of relaxation and festivity at the end of harvest. If, however, their extra children are to be fed then the extra crops must be grown.

As agriculture improves, increased rewards in crop yields are accompanied by increased losses should the crop be destroyed by pests or diseases. After doubling the rice yields, IRRI therefore concentrated on pest and disease resistance. The latest strains escape or resist two or more major pests and five or six of the main diseases of rice. This is an unending battle, since the new variety which avoids attack by, say a plant hopper, in the international series of trials, may always prove susceptible to a different species or even a different strain of pest, which may build up populations to attack it. The new varieties are regarded by scientists as a

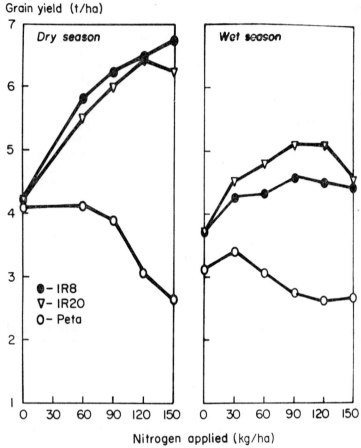

Fig. 2.   New rice varieties, with and without fertilisers. Data are averages for 1968–1973
cropping seasons at four locations. (*Source: International Rice Research Institute*, 1974).

contribution towards increasing food supplies of the countries concerned,
but not as a solution to the world's problems. It is unfortunate that
popular discussion has tended to exaggerate both the successes and the
failures of the new varieties from IRRI and CIMMYT.

IRRI is continuing the work for rice varieties capable of overcoming
special problems of rice farmers, such as saline soils, acid soils, coldwater
or deep water, or even periodic flooding. The Institute has a wide remit,
and has done valuable work in developing small motor tillers to work in
paddy fields; another very useful practical development has been small
cheap threshing machines.

Very interesting recent progress has been made with multiple cropping systems in which rice alternates with beans, groundnuts, maize, etc. Mixed cropping, in which two different crops are grown in alternate rows, has been shown to have advantages in pest and disease control. A vigorous 'outreach programme' has introduced improved rice strains throughout Asia, Africa and Latin America. That new varieties should survive in this vast range of ecological patterns in which rice farmers work around the world is surprising enough; that they should have increased yields significantly almost everywhere they have been tried, is a genuine triumph for the application of science to agriculture. Through CGIAR, 14 international donors support IRRI.

IITA (International Institute for Tropical Agriculture)
This was the next centre to be established, beginning in 1965. It has the specific remit to improve the agriculture of the humid tropics of Africa. The principal target is the 'shifting cultivation' system. This provides modest sustenance where small populations inhabit large areas of tropical forest or scrubland. As populations have grown, rest periods for regeneration of soil fertility have become too short and the output is declining rapidly.

Sited near Ibadan in Nigeria, the development of IITA was somewhat handicapped by the civil war but it has already made very useful contributions to African agriculture. The tropical root crops, the yams and cassava and the tropical legumes, particularly the cowpea (*Vigna unguiculata*) have already responded to intensive improvement, especially in resistance to pests and diseases. Soya beans, maize and rice from other centres, and indeed from many other countries, have been assembled and selected for local conditions. Plant breeding has begun for local adaptation.

A great deal of tropical soil science had already been developed and applied by the colonial service in Nigeria; IITA has built on this to make rapid progress with the maintenance of soil fertility. It has a large training wing and a continuous flow of African colleagues; both students and mature scientists come for residential courses and for seminars.

CIAT (International Centre for Tropical Agriculture)
In 1968 another centre was established to improve the agricultural output of the humid lowland tropics of South America. Here vast areas of empty grasslands in the foothills of the Andes are at present unused because of their acid leached soils and their long dry season. The grass is so poor in nutrients that cattle starve and fail to breed. The population live on very poor crops of beans, maize and cassava, with a few hardy pigs which scavenge for what they can find. Beef, swine, cassava, beans and maize are therefore the CIAT remit with the overriding objective to create viable farming systems which can use this vast land resource. Only a very few

years of intensive work with international support has enabled CIAT to show that African tropical legumes, of which the most successful is Stylo (*Stylosanthes* species), can survive these soils and can support productive beef cattle of hardy tropical zebu breeds.

CIP (International Potato Centre)
Higher up in the Andes, in Peru, the International Potato Centre has been established in the botanical home of the potato, where there is an immense variety of wild potato species and strains. Here the potato blight (*Phytophthera infestans*), the same blight which afflicts potato crops all over the world is also indigenous. There has been ample opportunity during their botanical history for the wild potatoes to develop resistance to blight and they are a fertile source of new breeding material.

ICRISAT (International Centre for Research in the Semi Arid Tropics)
This also was set up in 1972, and is the Centre dealing with crop research in those countries in which rainfall is too erratic for wheat, maize or even barley and the populations depend for their carbohydrates on sorghums and millets and for their proteins on the deep-rooted pigeon peas, the quick-growing chickpea or the highly productive groundnut (peanut). It is sited at Hyderabad in southern India. Plant improvement on all five crops is making good initial progress, even before the laboratories are built. Shaping the land to make the best use of scarce rainfall is the first stage in improving agriculture. Soil and water conservation methods have been well developed in the USA and have been adapted in East and Central Africa to tropical soils, but their combinations with improved crops into viable farming systems is an essential target for international science and ICRISAT has a major task in the international programme.

ILRAD (International Laboratory for Research into Animal Diseases)
This was set up only last year in Nairobi, Kenya, to study two major cattle diseases of Africa. These are Trypanosomiasis carried by the tsetse fly and East Coast Fever carried by cattle ticks.

ILCA (International Livestock Centre for Africa)
This was set up, also last year, to study and assist with livestock production schemes under a wide variety of conditions in the many countries of Africa. On the rolling savannahs, the semi-desert plains or the wet mountain slopes, whether these are inhabited by nomads or by settled villagers, there is a general need to earn money from the livestock in order to pay for the medicine and education which these populations are learning to value. This centre has been in rather stormy weather, since it was set up just outside Addis Ababa immediately before the overthrow of the imperial regime, but it has survived and is going ahead with its difficult task.

A further centre, ICARDA, is still in the process of initiation to serve the dryland agriculture of the Middle East.

A special laboratory for developing fertiliser formulations for use in the tropics has been set up at the Tennessee Valley Authority's headquarters in order to use their unique facilities: this is funded at present by the USA. The World Bank is increasing its programme of construction of fertiliser manufacturing plants in the developing countries as the international centres emphasise the importance of plant nutrition in crop production.

THE POPULATION PROBLEM

The combination of bilateral aid from many developed countries and the powerful system of international centres, together represent a major world effort to apply science to the improvement of agricultural production in the tropics and in particular to improvement of the life and farming skills of the subsistence farmer. The other side of the balance between population and food supply has, however, had all too little attention. The biggest obstacle to progress is the sheer poverty which persists in those areas where population increase continuously cancels out improvement in agriculture (Fig. 3). It is well established that both tradition and the economics of poverty among subsistence cultivators weigh heavily against restrictions on the size of families, but this is not the end of the argument. Traditional village life is already being destroyed in many tropical countries by the sheer pressure of population on a limited land resource. New generations are growing up under circumstances in which they may well prefer

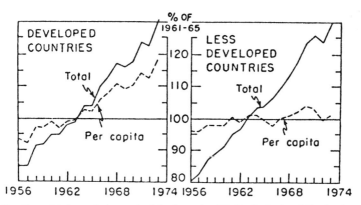

Fig. 3. Growth of population and of food supply. World Agricultural Production. The developed countries include the USA, Canada, Europe, USSR, Japan, South Africa, Australia and NZ. The less developed countries include Latin America, Asia (except Japan and communist countries) and Africa (except SA). (Poleman, 1975).

102 H. C. PEREIRA

the option of small families if given acceptable means to achieve it, but the control of human fertility is a subject in which science has been, and still is, inhibited by cultural, emotional and religious constraints. Science has not yet made the progress necessary to enable poor people of little education to adopt family planning, even if a new generation should become convinced that it is desirable. Here again the great Foundations have had the foresight to support work which may well make major contributions to the quality of life in the coming century.

THE UPTAKE OF SCIENCE

Although the time is short, the major task of improving the efficiency of tropical crop production, up to the levels already achieved for temperate crops, can certainly be accomplished and research and development aspects are now receiving a fair measure of attention and effort. The problems of promoting the improved crops, and the improved 'packages' of methods needed for high yields so that they are rapidly adopted in practice by the farmers of the developing world, remain to be solved. It is largely a matter of political will among the peoples and the governments concerned.

The new $5000 million International Fund for Agricultural Development, to be raised by the World Food Council, based on FAO, could be a major help in accelerating progress. Dr Boerma, addressing the World Food Conference, said that only 10% of international aid funds had been spent on agriculture. A much greater priority for food production is now essential for survival.

It is salutary to remember that Virgil's *Georgics*, written over 2000 years ago, described rotations of cereals and legumes in a crude and laborious, but effective system of agriculture. The Romans brought to Britain a farming system which was superior to that now used by the majority of the subsistence cultivators in the developing countries of the tropical world. That massive timelag of 2000 years is set in stark contrast to the world's race with time as the population doubles in the remaining 24 years of this century.

REFERENCES

Dalrymple, D. G. (1975). *USDA Foreign Agric. Econ. Rep.* No. 106.
International Rice Research Institute (1974). Annual Report.
Ministry of Agriculture, Fisheries and Food (1968). *A Century of Agricultural Statistics: Great Britain* 1866–1966, HMSO, London.
Ministry of Agriculture, Fisheries and Food. *Annual Reviews of Agriculture*, HMSO, London.
Poleman, T. T. (1975). *Science*, **188**, 510–518.

CHAPTER 10

Food from farm to table

J. B. M. COPPOCK

Spillers Limited

The title of this contribution was chosen carefully. It seeks to avoid perpetuating the artificial barrier of the farm gate as the place where food research begins. A barrier which, except in monetary terms, the second Reports of the Boards of the Joint Consultative Organisation for Research and Development (Ministry of Agriculture, Fisheries and Food, 1975b) recognise and do much to remove. These reports, make it clear that, in order to obtain best results, the food processor requires well defined characteristics in the primary raw materials he buys from the farmer, whether they be cereal or root crops, legumes, horticultural crops or animals and poultry pre-slaughter. They also recognise that the maximisation of yields and desirable processing characteristics do not always go together.

With animals and poultry it is now understood that immediate pre-slaughter conditions of stress (including adequacy in lairage hygiene, methods of killing and post-mortem handling of carcass meat from bleeding to final cold storage conditions) can have profound effects on meat quality. It is also recognised that farming practices such as the quality of the husbandry and the selection and feeding of stock are important both to satisfy the technological demands of the processor and the wishes of the consumer, whether the end-product is eaten directly as meat or indirectly as processed foods.

At the other end of the food chain, *i.e.* at the point of alimentary absorption and afterwards, the human nutritionist finds himself considerably involved in what happens both before and after the farm gate. Nowadays, neither the plant nor animal nutritionist can escape from involvement with the food processors' and the consumers' requirements. He is no longer solely concerned with the physiological requirements of his charges, but must be aware that different genetic material can produce different end-products, which must be suitable for the purpose to which they are to be put. He is therefore in turn dependent on the geneticist and the plant or animal breeder. The plant breeder can no longer select for yield alone; for example, he is soon told by the miller and baker that the new wheat varieties Maris Huntsman or Clement have α-amylase characteristics

103

which make them unsuitable for bread baking. The animal breeder must breed animals with a more favourable lean meat to fat ratio and in a configuration which best lends itself to producing the maximum number of the more popular cuts.

Thus the human nutritionist finds that he has incomplete control of the nutritional status of his subjects. He must be aware of the ways primary foods have been produced and the degree to which they have been affected during storage, distribution and subsequent processing in factory and home. He may find himself involved in the discussions of such bodies as the Committee on Medical Aspects of Food Policy (COMA) whose decisions may lead to legally defined nutritional standards, for example about the addition of chalk to flours other than wholemeal, of thiamin, iron and nicotinic acid to white flour, and the addition of vitamins A and D to margarine.

In the same context the recent report on novel proteins (Food Standards Committee, 1974) recognises that nutritional problems can arise if simulated meat products, based on oil seed proteins such as soya, replace a significant amount of meat in our diet. The addition of methionine to such products is advocated (although the method of choice avoiding off flavour development is not disclosed) and fortification with iron, thiamin, riboflavin and vitamin B_{12}, because of a relative lack of these nutrients compared with meat.

These preliminary observations by no means exhaust the complexity of any discussions on food from farm to table. The housewife is concerned with the farmers' use of pesticides, insecticides, herbicides, hormones and non-medical antibiotics as growth stimulants in animal and poultry feeding and fears the residues she believes might contaminate her foods. And this is before the food processor makes use of food additives as technological aids or cosmetic additions, which she learns from the media to be a description of food colours.

Food uneaten, for whatever reason, has no nutritional value; food acceptability is therefore of prime importance and this to the housewife means wholesome and safe food. The industrial revolution, has created conurbations of population which can only be fed by highly sophisticated farming and food production methods, including all forms of preservation from spoilage. It is of little use telling the housewife this unless we convince her that modern practices produce food as safe, wholesome and tasty, as she believes her grandparents and parents enjoyed.

Thus at a number of points in the food chain the analytical chemist and the toxicologist are needed to satisfy the housewife, and the general public, that current farming and food processing methods do not involve additional hazards to health. One of the currently disconcerting facts is the lack of young scientists coming forward with adequate training in food analysis, a matter clearly revealed in a survey recently made of the graduate requirements of food companies in the UK (J. B. M. Coppock, unpublished). The risk that public anxiety could divert research efforts from more useful aspects of production is mentioned in the report of the Food Science and Technology Board (1975) as follows: 'a further factor which has recently influenced the pattern of food research is consumer and public attitudes to possible toxic hazards in foods, the use of food additives and the possible presence in foods of environmental contaminants. The elimination of all hazards in food consumption is not possible if only because naturally occurring constituents may be toxic. Unreasonable demands by the public (and the news media) quite disproportionate to actual risks incurred which should be compared with the much higher risks from other hazards of modern life, could direct research effort from improving the quantity, quality and value of raw and processed foods, to fruitless efforts to assess the significance of very remote risks arising from the possible presence of toxic substances'.

These problems are not helped by various popularly written books by members of the medical profession. One recent example (Mackmarness, 1976) put forward the case for allergies to chemicals added to foods, or to food processing methods. The plethora of clinical material on psychiatric and other abnormal patients makes it difficult to assess the real from the imagined. Medical opinions should not be confused with medical facts. Some might well suggest that epidemiological studies are necessary to assess whether there is truth in the belief that natural foods are better for us than processed foods, but again such studies could well divert research funds from more useful objectives.

Nevertheless the Food Science and Technology Board does recognise that 'there is little understanding of how consumers see nutritional issues or what determines their preferences for particular foods. Changes in food habits are brought about by new product introduction (which includes the influence of advertising) as well as by economic constraints and social changes'. These aspects were commented on briefly in the Agricultural Research Council/Medical Research Council report (1974) and the observation was made that little is known on how nutritionally desirable changes in consumers' food habits can be suggested and accepted. This might be of great importance if the world population explosion, coupled with the escalating cost of energy and its potential shortage by 2000 A.D., makes changes necessary in our national food consumption pattern and the Board wisely recommends that further research is required on what determines public attitudes to food.

Clearly food research resources must be expended with care and so far, compared with agriculture, they are not large. In 1974, publicly funded research programmes amounted to about £3·6 million per annum on food compared to £38·9 million for agriculture and £3·1 million for fisheries. It is not surprising that the Food Science and Technology Board comments that the 'correct division of resource for R and D between the three inter-related areas of food, agriculture and fisheries requires assessment against the criterion of real future needs, without undue reference to the past or even present patterns of expenditure. These patterns have not arisen as the result of conscious overall planning but of uncoordinated decisions of several government departments'. From reading these reports one suspects that the farm gate was a barrier in these decisions but hopes that in future more of the agricultural expenditure will be directed towards study of the qualities in raw materials required by the processor and the consumer.

It would be unfair however to create the impression that progress has not already been made. Consumer and industrial pressures have fed back to the farmer and grower vital information on raw material quality. Thus we have already seen in both beef and pork quality higher lean meat/fat ratios and less fat bacon. The Meat Research Institute (1972) has held a conference bringing together international experience on cold shortening (toughness) in lamb and other meats. The canners of peas, beans and other vegetables have demanded and obtained qualities essential for improved processing. The cultivation and storage problems of the Cox apple in comparison with those of its continental competitor, Golden Delicious, have stimulated the production of a new variety, Suntan, by the East Malling Research Station. Strawberry cultivars more suitable for canning have been developed in collaboration with the Campden Food Preservation Research Association.

In terms of energy output to input ratios cereals are very important food sources. Because they can rely considerably on photosynthesis for their growth they utilise solar energy very efficiently and so have energy output to input ratios greater than unity. Grains generally have a value of about two according to Blaxter (1975) and Leach (1975). There are also differences between cereals, the value for wheat, 2·3, being greater than that for barley, 1·8.

Bread, with an output/input ratio of 1·4 is clearly a very valuable food. Potatoes have a ratio of unity, sugar beet 0·5, battery eggs 0·16, broiler poultry 0·11 with meat somewhat lower, *i.e.* over 20 times less than for wheat. Sea fishing is, however, very energy intensive, having a ratio of 0·073 which means nearly 15 energy units of fossil fuel are used, nearly all of it from oil, for each unit of energy eaten. Some might argue that the £3·1 million of public money spent on fisheries research is unrealistic in view of these energy considerations. One cannot accept this, however, knowing of the work being done by Burgess and his colleagues (Burgess, 1975) on the significant addition which could be made to our fish supplies by blue whiting and red fish, or a more ready acceptance of the mackerel. The problems lie in attempting to change conservative British attitudes to fish choice, which if more flexible could significantly contribute to our protein needs.

Protein yields in terms of energy input are a little less unfavourable for animal products; for instance compared with 45 MJ/kg of protein for wheat, the energy input in MJ/kg is 2·5 times greater for milk, 7·7 for beef, 5·2 for pork, 4·4 for eggs and broiler meat. Wheat again is favoured with 45 MJ/kg compared with 58 MJ/kg for barley. Nevertheless, in relation to the land area employed both the energy and protein output, however calculated, are significantly greater for arable crops than for animal products. This should cause no surprise since animals fed on plants are bound to produce less energy as meat than that contained in the plants consumed.

On such calculations some argue that it is wasteful to consume meat, when protein can be, in terms of energy, and in real economic terms, more cheaply obtained from plant sources including oil seeds such as soya. Some supplementation in our diet by such proteins for meat will inevitably take place but it may well be wrong to assume animal production will remain as energy expensive as at present. Blaxter has suggested that far better use could be made of pasture, of forage and of leaf protein (Blaxter, 1975); experiments in Aberdeen have demonstrated that monogastric animals, such as pigs, can use pressed leaf juice as a protein source, whilst ruminants can successfully utilise the fibrous residue still containing protein and available to cattle and sheep. There appear to be rich rewards from transferring the properties of nitrogen fixation from bacteria to crop species, or to bacterial species which are often components of the soil and root area of crops. In addition, and this may require some education of the consumer, waste products such as dried poultry manure and ruminant faeces can provide important sources of crude protein for ruminant feeding.

Less difficult from a social point of view will be exploitation in animal feeds of municipal waste, cellulose rich wastes (bagasse, waste paper, straw) and other carbohydrate rich wastes such as molasses and date stones. Rape seed too could prove a useful crop as it has in Canada, as the plant breeders have successfully bred out the toxic substance erucic acid in new rape varieties. It is not beyond expectation that they may rid the protein of some of the toxic substances still causing anxiety. For reasons of this kind the JCO Agricultural Board expressed some reservations on the utilisation of oil seed rape by the feedingstuffs industry, although the working groups on protein crops gave research on oil seed rape priority over lupins, peas, linseed, sunflower and the soya bean. Perhaps the Board had in mind that we should grow those crops that we know grow well in our climate. Such thinking is in line with the recent government White Paper, *Food from Our Own Resources* (Ministry of Agriculture, Fisheries and Food, 1975a). For example, a policy to reduce North American wheat imports and to replace them by home grown and EEC wheat makes sense and a working party has been set up by the Food Science and

Technology Board to consider whether changes in milling and baking techniques will be required to do this and to investigate the value of new wheat varieties. Of interest at the 'table' however will be the nutritive value of the resulting bread and it is to be hoped that the protein content of bread will not suffer too much by the replacement of the higher protein containing wheats of North America, by British and European varieties with lower protein contents.

The Board would appear to have a duty to the housewife and the public in matters of this kind, for the safeguarding of nutritional quality is clearly stated as one of its aims. The food technologist too requires reminding about what his processes can do to nutritional value, and this responsibility is inherent in the recent professional conduct guidelines on the wholesomeness of food drawn up by the UK Institute of Food Science and Technology for its members. The consumers' attitude to technological change in food production cannot be ignored and in instances where government policy initiates researches into staple foods it is all the more essential that government takes some responsibility in educating the public on new methods and new food needs whenever they arise.

To what kind of conclusion do the various complexities lead us. It seems that apart from the dependence of agriculture and food processing on the basic sciences of biology, chemistry and physics, the length of the food chain is increasing and becoming even more dependent on these basic disciplines. It might be thought trite briefly to look back 50 years and more to the food in our larders then. It is my recollection that the sack of flour sometimes harboured mice, that the bread staled more rapidly than now and that one was told not to eat it when it was warm (and the most delectable) because it would cause indigestion. With all the care which good cooks command sometimes the homemade jam and bottled fruit became mouldy; this surface mould was scraped off (dangerous mycotoxins were then unknown) and the remainder was cheerfully consumed. Many other foods spoiled too. Milk was regarded as a particular problem, not only did it sour in summer but there was the constant anxiety that it was not tubercle free. How many people who condemn processed foods now realise the contribution pasteurisation and the new methods of ultra high temperature treatment have had on removing this fear? All these problems occurred in a farming district in which were the traditional bakery, grocer's shop and butchers' shop with the meat killed on the premises. Food hygiene was minimal and one accepted mild doses of food poisoning as ordinary hazards of life. No one had heard of salmonella poisoning from consuming duck eggs, although one was sometimes warned about potential ptomaine poisoning from imperfectly canned products, particularly meats. Thus although generally (with certain obvious exceptions) the food chain was then short, it was imperfect, and the need for better methods of food preservation including refrigeration was clear. One became aware of imported meat being acceptable after transport in the holds of refrigerated ships. The pioneering work in Glasgow on refrigeration, by the Bell brothers and Coleman was known.

The emphasis on technology in the US had caused that country to be somewhat ahead of the UK, just as it is now in its more sophisticated approach to quality assurance, including nutritional labelling, and the development of advanced methods for testing textural and other sensory qualities which the US regards as a greater part of in-line factory quality control than we do in this country.

Product development and market research in the UK tends too often to be product orientated regarding potential use and purchase, and there is scant attention to nutritional value. Some would say that in the US too, marketing men, when moving from convenience foods to 'empty calorie' fun foods, also lost sight of nutritional value. There are many pitfalls in product development.

The physiology of taste and odour is still much neglected and the housewife and the general public may well be excused if they still echo the views of George Orwell in *The Road to Wigan Pier* (first published in 1937): 'To begin with, there is the frightful debauchery of taste that has already been effected by a century of mechanisation—take taste in its narrowest sense, the taste of decent food. In the highly mechanised countries, thanks to tinned food, cold storage, synthetic flavouring matters, etc. the palate is almost a dead organ.' Greater efforts are clearly required to educate the consumer on the need for modern methods; for the alternative may be starvation.

The consumer is little aware of the care the food manufacturer takes. Jam-making, an area in which the housewife believes she reigns supreme can be taken as an illustration. Harrison (1974) has described some of the jam manufacturers' criteria. With strawberries, it can be an advantage to have a cultivar in which the colour extends throughout the berry rather than having it confined to the outer layers. Variations in colour can be even greater, depending on differing degrees of ripeness or harvesting conditions. The jam manufacturer looks for fruit free from blemish by disease, mildew, pests or adverse weather. Dark markings on the skins of oranges and peaches are most troublesome. Fruit size is also important. Fruit that is too small can reduce production rates, as found when destalking strawberries by hand and fruit that is too large can cause feed lines to block. There were problems in the 1950s in making jam in season from the strawberry variety 'Brenda' which could not be penetrated by sugar so that the berry stayed whole. The strawberry could float with lowering of soluble solids at the surface, and this could affect keeping quality. The new variety, 'Cambridge Favourite', has the opposite effect and indeed tends if anything to break down all too readily. Thus there is still room for improvement in the cultivar.

Undesirable toughness due to enzyme activity in cold storage can develop in certain fruits like damsons and blackcurrants. In this context it must be remembered that although fruit production is seasonal, jam production is not. Thus in some sulphited fruits, notably strawberries, the fruit has been known to break down completely due to the presence of certain fungi which can live in acid conditions. Acidity, pectin content and chemical constitution, which aid gel formation, are of great importance and so is the rate of set. Adjustment of acidity is important and is normally in the range pH 3·0–3·5. Small additions of fruit acids lower pH and increase the rate of set; the addition of sodium bicarbonate in the boiling process increases pH and lowers the setting rate. Set is also affected by the soluble solids in the jam and its temperature at the time of filling the jar or can. These quality factors are continuously monitored.

The five factors mentioned above in controlling set are also of importance in preventing a poor appearance developing in a jam, from machine filling turbulence causing air bubble formation. These must have time to disperse. On the other hand if set is too long delayed in jams containing whole fruit, then the fruit can either rise or sink with convection currents within the jar. This is particularly seen in marmalade when the orange shreds will distribute themselves in uneven patterns if the set is incorrect.

When the jar containing hot jam has been sealed it is cooled, usually continuously on a wide belt bounded by pressure sprays of cool water. These sprays are directed at the cap rather than the jar, but this can cause a problem. The head space may develop a sharp drop in pressure, and if the filling temperature is high, can cause boiling of the jam under reduced pressure. This usually happens in the middle of the jar, causing changes during setting. In transparent jams bubbles which develop are noticeable and unsightly. These and many other quality control problems occur which cannot be seen and if the jam is in a can, and not a jar, even more stringent controls are necessary. Finally flavour is very important. This is often related to the cultivar used; the flavour differences between wild and cultivated fruits are well known. When preserved fruit is used the methods of preservation and storage have important effects on flavour. With plum jam, where all the other aspects, including flavour are right, the plum itself may possess a stone which splinters in the jam making process.

This description of some of the problems in jam-making illustrates very clearly that food processing cannot be divorced from issues on the other side of the farm gate. The creation of the Ministry of Agriculture, Fisheries and Food has done much to remove this artificial barrier and the responsibility of the Ministry for research in all sectors of agriculture and food is of immense benefit to consumer and industry alike. Those of us who recognise the value of the various Boards of the JCO see liaison between the Boards as vital to the appreciation in agricultural circles that specific crop, cultivar, or livestock qualities are essential to good food processing. The ARC/MRC report on Food and Nutrition Research (1974) and the second report of the Food Science and Technology Board of the JCO are complementary. Taken together they cover most aspects of current and future UK research and development problems associated with food from farm to table. There are three areas where some small criticisms can be made. The first criticism is that neither report takes the question of the kind of research needed to learn more of the social implications of food and nutrition habits much further nor discusses how such work could be better financed. Food flavour is certainly part of the problem; if agricultural yields are alone considered this may be acceptable to the flavourist (B. M. Coppock, 1975), but will it satisfy the housewife—for flavour and yield are not synonymous? Secondly, it gives no guide to the exploration that should be made into the use of more exotic animals which might contribute to the animal protein problem. For example, the eland has potential value because of its ability to eat leaves widely available in various parts of Africa. Thirdly, in these times of convenience eating, it is of some importance that not only should the nutritional aspects of manufactured foods be considered, but also those of catering practices. The technical operations of the catering industry do not seem to have been considered as part of the Food Science and Technology Board's original remit, but it is clear that nowadays they form a most essential part of food research and development. The pioneering work done at Leeds University in institutional catering and the pilot experiment now under way in Newcastle upon Tyne will provide evidence on how well the nutritional status of a wide section of the public can be maintained on depot frozen foods, providing that there is a good menu variety and that foods are reheated appropriately after distribution, although George Orwell would think it abhorrent.

Nevertheless, we must appreciate that there are few reserves in the world food larder, and that methods of this kind, which can also be designed significantly to reduce food waste, may be essential if food and energy possibly become simultaneous problems. The average solar energy falling on a square metre of British soil is about 50 W daily. Man operates on about 150 W, of which he radiates about 40 W daily. If we could perfectly capture and utilise all the energy falling on the size of a hearthrug our problems could be solved. The scope for the biologist is clearly immense, and one will expect ideas totally different from current views on the use of algae which absorb solar energy, or the consumption of the relatively energy expensive single cell proteins, to emerge. There are other areas of self help, and the application of simple physical principles can do much. Photosynthesis still seems to remain the key, and improving the efficiency of our farming processes is our main hope with the development of new kinds. Is it fanciful to observe that mussels provide far more protein than an equivalent area sown with wheat? One does not necessarily have to eat shellfish to obtain the protein; methods of extracting bland fish proteins are already known.

Internationally an understanding of the interaction of soil and climate is of particular importance for the next advance in agricultural productivity. Climate may be beyond our control, but as Sir Joseph Hutchinson (1973) prophetically said just prior to the energy crisis, the management of soil and crop variety so that they conform to climatic limitations is the essence of husbandry. A clear example is the development of triticale, the wheat rye cross (J. B. M. Coppock, 1975), with its yield potential in arid areas. With the control of fertility now available to us, husbandry has entered a new phase. Photosynthesis is its basis, but man's ingenuity still remains the stimulant. Thus one of the most exciting prospects is that of integrating fertility level and crop duration with the management of monsoon water, thereby creating a high production agriculture in India where rain and solar energy are abundant.

Is it too philosophical to conclude that whereas now we have to demonstrate technological need for new food additives, the three problems of population explosion, the growing energy shortage from fossil fuels, and food supplies, could mean that within a century we may have to seek government approval by demonstrating nutritional value as a prerequisite to the development of any new processed food product?

REFERENCES

Agricultural Research Council/Medical Research Council (1974). *Food and Nutrition Research*, Report of the ARC/MRC committee, HMSO, London.

Blaxter, K. L. (1975). 'The energetics of British agriculture', *J. Sci. Fd. Agric.*, **26**, 1055.

Burgess, G. H. O. (1975). 'Fish in the nation's diet', *BNF Bulletin*, **3**, 27.

Coppock, B. M. (1975). A Study of Beef Flavour, PhD Thesis, p. 17, University of London.

Coppock, J. B. M. (1975). 'Triticale', *Nutrition and Food Science*, No. 39, p. 15.

Food Standards Committee (1974). *Report on Novel Protein Foods*, HMSO, London.

Harrison, E. (1974). Chocolate and Sugar Confectionery and Preserves. In: *10th Anniversary Symposium of the UK Institute of Food Science and Technology*, p. 27, IFST, London.

Hutchinson, J. (1973). 'A discussion on agricultural productivity in the 1980s', *Phil. Trans. R. Soc. Ser. B*, **267**, 171.

Leach, G. (1975). *Energy and Food Production*, International Institute for Environment and Development, London and Washington D.C.

Mackmarness, R. (1976). *Not all in the Mind*, Pan Books, London.

Meat Research Institute (1972). *Meat Chilling, Why and How*, Symposium No. 2, Meat Research Institute, Langford, Bristol.

Ministry of Agriculture, Fisheries and Food (1975a). *Food from Our Own Resources*, Cmnd 6020, HMSO, London.

Ministry of Agriculture, Fisheries and Food (1975b). Second Reports of the Boards of the Joint Consultative Organisation for Research and Development in Agriculture and Food, HMSO, London.

CHAPTER 11

New food technologies and their role in the world

A. T. JAMES and D. W. LARBEY

Unilever Research, Colworth/Welwyn Laboratory, Sharnbrook, Bedford

Everywhere in the world food gathering and preparation is an integral part of social organisation. Generally, it means more to people than simply freedom from hunger. Age old practices of preserving food and making it more palatable such as drying, salting, fermenting, and cooking are ubiquitous and are considered to be culinary art and hence respectable, unlike more modern processes. Investigating and understanding the structure and activity of biological raw materials, and applying the knowledge to make food is a pursuit of the developed countries. Food science and technology develops from general scientific understanding and hence it is not surprising that most innovation in food production originates in the Western world, and therefore is geared to the needs of affluent industrialised society. Despite the economic crisis, people in the West are still well off. They have a relatively abundant and varied food supply drawn from all over the world and money to buy it. Eating problems are largely hedonistic, and consumers demand variety, sensuality and convenience in their foods, taking for granted high standards of manufacturing practices, safety and nutrition, which are in any case ensured by law. In the third world, needs are quite different and preservation and distribution are poorly operated. Populations are large, indigenous food production is frequently inefficient and there is little money. Their need is simply for more food on the table although even hungry people expect food to fit their long established dietary patterns. Because of the very great cultural differences, new technologies developed for western food systems are rarely appropriate to developing countries. Some advances in food technology expected to make a significant social impact in Britain in the next 15 years and some attempts to transfer technology or technological food products to developing countries illustrate this.

Britain is heavily dependent on imports for many agricultural raw materials and for oil. In recent years, world prices for these commodities have increased sharply, pushing the cost of food production to new levels. Supply is also a problem. Rising population and the pressure for higher living standards throughout the world are making increasing demands on the food available. All the indications are that in the 1980s less reliance can be placed on Britain's ability to purchase the raw materials that currently make up almost half the food supply. Much of the food imported could be grown in this country, and indeed self sufficiency in indigenous food materials has been increasing at a yearly rate of $2\frac{1}{2}\%$. However, future expansion of production will be confined to the 47 million acres of land already in use. Within this constraint there is no technological reason why expansion cannot be sustained. It requires that agricultural research continues to lead to increased yields of foodstuffs per acre, that wastage is decreased, and that farmers adopt new techniques as willingly as they have done in the past. As Britain strives to become more self reliant in food production including fish and fish products, the importance of food technology will necessarily increase. The basic role of the food processing industry is to transform the sometimes inedible and usually short lived raw materials produced by the farmer and fisherman into attractive, convenient and more palatable forms that will keep for long periods. Nowadays the emphasis in research and development is towards exploiting new raw materials, making better use of traditional crops, and energy conservation in processing.

NEW RAW MATERIALS

The animal feeds industry was originally based on the by-products of fat extraction of oil bearing crops. Oil seed cakes were mixed with cereals to form balanced rations for livestock. Now, edible oil producing countries use much of the by-products for their own livestock. Furthermore, modern solvent extraction techniques leave less oil in the meal than the old expeller-crush methods thereby decreasing its feed value. Consequently, the animal feeds industry has become an important consumer of cereals, the production of which was previously geared to human consumption. Thus in recent years animal feed compounders have used large quantities of raw materials which, with suitable processing could also be used by man. This and the fact that livestock are poor converters of energy and protein has led some people to suggest a potential conflict between man and his farm animals for the supply of food. Because of their unique digestive systems, cattle and sheep can use not only the fibrous raw materials unsuitable for monogastric animals including man, but also carbohydrates, fats and nitrogenous materials which are unsuitable for other species. Furthermore, large areas of the world geographically unsuited to any other form of agricultural production are useful for large scale cattle ranching. For these reasons, ruminants are not nearly so competitive with man as many people have made out. Nevertheless, there is a trend in the animal feeds industry to use side product raw materials which will make it complementary and not competitive with the human food system once again. Traditional vegetable protein sources will continue to supply part of future animal needs. However, there are new protein sources whose production will soon be expanded greatly. First, the recent technology of producing protein from single cell organisms grown on simple chemicals may be improved to result in a significant supply of economic biomass becoming available. Secondly, many higher plants, at present poorly used, are good sources of protein. It is already possible to extract protein from leaves and use it in the form of a highly concentrated powder as a feed ingredient in place of traditional fish meal and soya bean flour. The grass crop is an obvious one to exploit, but all leaves contain good quality protein and it may well be that in the future unfamiliar plants, even weeds, will outyield grass in this respect.

For energy, there are many crops that outyield cereals, the traditional carbohydrate crops for both animals and man. The really high yielders are tropical crops and most of them roots. Typical examples are yams, sweet potatoes and cassava, capable of producing up to 100 tons/hectare which is 15–20 times larger than a good cereal yield. Whether these are capable of being further developed as major food sources has yet to be determined.

With regard to fats and oils, the high value energy sources, we can rely on the skills of the chemist to process new types of oil seed and to improve yields of the tropical oil bearing crops.

Proteins, other than those from meat and milk, already feature in human food systems but a marked change in balance is expected in the next decade or so. The major alternative is of course soya protein. Single cell protein is unlikely to make any significant impact on the human diet for some time. Stringent standards for novel proteins are being passed into law and there are some toxicological problems to be surmounted before single cell protein can be produced for human consumption. (Even so, it has been estimated that production on a significant scale would require a capital investment equal to that already employed in the plastics industry.) Leaf protein has been around for many years but attempts to make it palatable have failed to such an extent that, in areas where people are starving, it has been difficult to give it away.

Protein from soya beans is quite different. The soya bean has been a traditional source of nutritious food in East Asia. The bean itself is not very suitable for consumption as such; it has to be boiled, fermented or extracted, that is processed in some way to make it palatable. Boiling produces off flavours, and the traditional products at their best, tempeh, tahoe, soy sauce, miso, etc., are not accommodated easily into the British way of life.

In the Western world soya beans are grown primarily for their oil, an important ingredient of margarine. The defatted meal remaining after oil extraction is toasted and used for animal feed. Recently, the merits of soya bean as a human food in the Western world has drawn considerable attention, particularly in the USA. The untoasted, defatted soya meal can be given a certain texture by extruding it. This material which has come to be known among other things as 'textured vegetable protein' gained popularity as a meat extender in 1972 when meat prices were high. However, sales declined the following year, and this was probably in part due to the off flavours which develop in products derived simply from defatted soya meal. Attempts to mask off flavours with other flavours can be effective, but now second generation products are available from which the less desirable materials, including those responsible for off flavours are removed. Either the less desirable materials are extracted and the proteins left behind in more concentrated form, consequently referred to as a 'concentrate', or the soluble proteins are extracted from the soya meal to form a so-called 'isolate'. Refined soya protein products have practically no nutritional drawbacks. There are even favourable features such as the absence of animal fat, low caloric value and the presence of indigestible polysaccharides, that is roughage, which may make them nutritionally desirable. The idea that textured vegetable protein simulating meat will quickly replace choice cuts in the market place has been dismissed long since, but they are being used increasingly as meat extenders in traditional products and provide raw material for new products which will add to variety without diminishing the nutritional value of the British diet.

In the EEC there is a move to establish oilseed rape as a source of both quality oil and palatable protein. Although only 1% of arable acreage is currently given to rape, its potential is very important. Whereas soya beans can be grown only in the southern areas of the Community, rape is the only satisfactory edible oilseed crop sufficiently developed for extensive cultivation in temperate climates. However, the toxic principles erucic acid and glucosinolate prevent its rapid acceptance, as also do the problems with pests and diseases. It is interesting in this respect that many growers in France are turning from rape to sunflower.

The search for new raw materials is not confined to vegetable sources. There is a search for larger leaner cattle both within and between breeds. Recently several exotic breeds have been introduced for evaluation under British conditions. Among them are the Blonde Aquitaine, Brown Swiss, Chianina, Gelbvieh, Maine Anjou, Murray Grey and Romagnola. Most of the native British breeds are of quite trivial numerical importance in beef production. By the same token few of the exotic breeds will establish a position for themselves. The Charolais has already done so, setting new standards for rate of lean beef production. The Simmental is already established having high performance but less calving difficulty than the Charolais. The Limousin seems likely to command respect as a breed with special carcass characteristics, in particular high muscle to bone ratio. For the rest, the future is uncertain. Probably the most important factor will be whether the breed can gain sufficient numerical strength to sustain a viable programme of genetic improvement. Meanwhile, commercial producers will experiment on a cautious scale.

Recent attempts have produced the Beefalo and The Yakow! Beefalo is three eighths buffalo, three eights Charolais and one quarter Hereford. Claims for it are 10% more protein, faster growth on grass alone, and better calving rates than conventional cattle. This means substantially less production costs and savings of 25% or more in retail prices. There are import restrictions to be overcome before live Beefalo are seen in Britain. However, we do have the Yakow, half Yak, half Scottish Highland which is being used to produce cattle more suited to the colder grasslands of Britain.

ELIMINATING WASTE

At all stages of food production from sowing seeds to the point of consumption there is considerable wastage of valuable food, amounting to as much as one third.

At harvest, much of the plant plays no part in utilisation of the crop. Cereal straw is burned, potato haulms are destroyed with acid, leafy tops are trimmed from root crops and pea vines are ploughed in. These crop residues have a significant food potential. There is also loss in the edible crop itself. Disease, damage, surplus and deterioration contribute to crop wastage. Further, there are processing losses both in the factories and at home.

Utilisation of such wastes can be seen at several levels of complexity. At the lowest level the farmer merely avoids disposal costs, with possibly some benefit. Straw burning and ploughing in pea vines fall into this category but by far the most common is sale for animal feed. Potatoes, wheat middlings, malt sprouts, brewers grains and sugar beet tops and pulp are examples. In theory, any waste which comprises non-toxic plant materials can be consumed beneficially as agricultural feed, but generally insufficient attention is given to the proper formulation of waste-derived feeds. A notable exception to this is the development in the use of straw for animal feeds.

The cereal crop in Britain is increasing. Currently, the straw is equivalent nutritionally to three million tons of barley grain, yet more than one third of it is burned and only up to one quarter is fed to animals. During the Second World War straw was steeped in caustic soda to break down the cell walls and improve its feed value for cattle, but because of the labour involved it has since lapsed into disfavour. Now, this one-time farm based process has been updated, mechanised and put on a factory basis, and interest in straw has been renewed. In feeding trials with dairy cows up to 30% of the traditional rations have been replaced with treated straw without affecting milk yield adversely. The economics of the process depends on the availability of straw. The first plant to be built in Britain's major cereal growing area processes four tons/hour and draws straw from anything up to 60 miles away. However, haulage of low density large volume loads is expensive and the success of the operation will depend to some extent on developing compression techniques for the straw.

Protein extracted from grass has already been mentioned as a novel animal feed but the extraction process works just as well for plant waste. In addition to the protein fraction a cellulosic one is produced. This is of little value by itself but it can be hydrolysed to sugars which in turn can be converted microbiologically to single cell protein. In this type of process, vegetable waste is not the only suitable raw material. There are strong indications that many organic wastes arising in large concentrations like domestic waste, sewage sludge, wood waste and farm waste can serve as feedstock for single cell protein. In these processes economy of scale is of paramount importance.

Complete fractionation of food waste is the most refined approach. Effluents from food processing factories are in most cases complex mixtures of chemicals potentially capable of being fractionated into a number of high value products. Although it will be many years before the processes are perfected, some significant developments have already been made. Protein can be removed from whey by ultrafiltration, from abattoir wastes by ion exchange and from potato processing effluent by heat coagulation.

Not all food recovered from waste is as unappetising as straw, sugar beet pulp or powdered proteins. In food processing factories enormous quantities of high quality meat and fish go to waste after prime cuts have been taken from the carcass. New techniques for stripping the bones, pulping the flesh and moulding it into forms suitable for inclusion in convenience products are playing an increasingly significant role in food conservation. On the farms fresh produce is rejected because its size, shape, colour or some other attribute is not to the consumer's liking. Similarly these can be pulped and reformed into high quality products that are acceptable. Processed apple segments, blackcurrants and other fruits are already available as pie fillings as a result of this technology.

Exploitation of new raw materials and efficient use of all food sources is only part of the changing scene. New developments in preservation, packaging, storage, distribution and retailing are closely linked, and together are transforming traditional food systems in Europe. Overall the trend is towards ambient stable products which avoid the cost of low temperature storage.

Milk is an example. Britain's daily doorstep milk delivery in glass bottles is unique, but it is part of the British way of life that may have to go. Even when the slump is over the permanently altered energy pattern will compel a drastic streamlining of distribution techniques. Large scale distribution must by its nature be more energy and labour intensive than large scale production. Economies of scale do not operate to anything like the same extent in distribution as they do in manufacturing, and it is inevitable that a distribution system which made sense in times when energy and labour were cheap cannot be viable when they are very expensive. An alternative method of milk distribution pioneered in France is based on ultra high temperature (UHT) pasteurisation. Milk is heated to very high temperatures for two or three seconds, and then packed into cartons aseptically. UHT milk is a high quality product with a good taste. It does not need refrigerating and has a shelf life of eight weeks or more. In France, UHT milk is distributed through hypermarkets. The package is strong enough to permit handling and storage without conventional returnable dairy cases. They are preassembled at the dairy into unit loads in roll containers on one-way shippers and then palletised and distributed to the hypermarket. In the store they are displayed as they arrive and placed where consumers can select for themselves. In this type of distribution system the trend is to shift more and more work from the retail outlet to the manufacturer thereby bypassing the wholesaler and reducing the need for staff to unpack and display. These savings and the fact that hypermarkets are placed out of town where rates are low, allows them to operate at lower margins.

Another development having a significant impact in Europe is flexible packaging, especially the so-called retortable pouches. These are an extension of the 'boil in bag' concept familiar in Britain with frozen products. Basically, they are flexible pouches of aluminium laminated inside and out with suitable plastics, which can be filled, emptied of air and sealed. Since the pouches contain a minimum of air or liquor and they conform closely to the shape of the product, the heat treatment required to sterilise is milder than with cans. Products can be of better quality both organoleptically and nutritionally because of this. In addition the geometry of the packs allows savings in energy, storage and distribution costs.

The overall trend in food preservation is towards milder processing. Rather than relying on one severe treatment to repress microbiological spoilage, combinations of less severe treatments are being developed. Intermediate moisture foods (IMF) are an example. These are characterised by water activity low enough to prevent the growth of bacteria and by conditions minimising the potential for growth of other micro-organisms.

Dried fruits, jams, some types of sausage and pie fillings are traditional intermediate moisture foods but a renaissance of IMF technology is under way. Typically, glycerol, sucrose, glucose or salt is used to lower water activity in combination with antimicrobial agents such as propylene glycol and sorbic acid. Stability may be increased by evaporation, pasteurisation, chemical preservatives and blanching. Application of this technology to pet foods, providing the 'soft-moist' or 'semi-moist' varieties has already been very successful.

FOOD TECHNOLOGY AND THE DEVELOPING COUNTRIES

Food technology in Western countries aims at continuing the provision of the variety and quality of food products that consumers have come to expect. It is capital intensive and operates on a scale not suitable for developing countries. In the third world the need is for more food and the money to buy it. In general this means a marked increase in agricultural production, application of low technology preservation processes using labour intensive methods and improved distribution.

Western technology influences the food systems in developing countries but not always to their advantage. Massive aid programmes that have distributed products of western food technology such as dried skim milk, corn-soy milk, and wheat-soy blends have had limited success because the foods are not easily accommodated by the traditional culture of the intended recipients. The food scientists and technologists trained in the industrialised countries have learnt how to fulfil the hedonistic desires of affluent people in temperate zones rather than the simpler needs of hungry people in subtropical and tropical countries. Too much of the food produced in developing countries goes to waste on the farm, in the markets and storage depots, and in the home. Proper food storage, processing and packaging could make much more food available and encourage farmers to produce more. All countries have developed their own food craft, that is experience with making foods more stable or palatable and in fact usually employ the simplest technologies, like sun drying, fermenting, and pickling. It is these areas, which are part of the culture, which need scientific development so that the improved methods and products remain substantially within the accepted culture of the people concerned.

Much of the intermediate technology available is not suitable for direct transfer to developing countries. Canning for example is an extremely practical way to extend the availability, convenience and safety of indigenous food supplies, but lack of available containers and high cost are serious economic barriers to the production of processed foods in developing countries. Manufacturing containers locally would be an answer but there is no equipment available which is suitable for developing countries.

Packaging technology is highly innovative, geared towards higher production rates and increased automation, and is capital intensive. Developing countries need machines to fit into labour intensive operations that are less capital intensive. Solutions to problems such as this could mean recycling the ideas of earlier days in the development of western technology.

In spite of deep roots in traditional food systems, and proximity to hunger, developing countries will undoubtedly tend towards western style eating. The desire to enjoy more and better food, when such can be afforded is universal. The correlation between the gross domestic product *per caput* and consumption of food energy is well known. Generally, consumers are the final arbiter of any innovation in the food industry. They eat what they like to eat. In the UK 500 new food products are promoted nationally each year yet within five years half of these disappear from the market. Such is the desire of well fed people for new food varieties, and their capacity for rejecting those they do not like.

Similar trends can be seen in developing countries. Sorely needed nutritional products distributed free in food aid programmes have met with only limited acceptance. On the other hand, other sophisticated food products have an ill defined yet potent ability to change accepted custom, which can be dangerous with a largely uneducated population. Foods such as ice cream, fish fingers and cornflakes are enjoyed by many non-western consumers.

Though developing countries offer limited potential markets for high technology foods, in the short term exposure to such products will set trends for the ultimate development of an indigenous sophisticated food industry.

CHAPTER 12

Future trends in the use of protein resources

J. MAURON

Nestlé Products Technical Assistance Co. Ltd

INTRODUCTION

Is it not rather odd that the great research effort made during the last two decades or so to develop new sources of protein has its origin in an assumption which in the meantime has been shown to be wrong? Indeed, there is, for the time being, no real protein gap in the world, in the sense that minimal physiological protein requirements cannot be met. It is true that there are vulnerable groups that do not cover their protein needs in their daily food but this is generally due to lack of food and not specifically to lack of protein. Even in populations relying on starchy roots such as manioc as the staple food, typical protein malnutrition in the form of kwashiorkor is not a general phenomenon, but is limited to infants and young mothers of the socially most deprived sections of the population. This is due to the fact that the protein requirements of man are relatively low so that for the adult the minimum needs are met even with very poor diets as long as enough of the latter is eaten.

As an example I present the results of the dietary survey I made in a village of the Kwilu province, in one of the poorest sections of Zaire using the exact weighing method (Mauron, to be published). In a typical family, adult protein intake did not exceed 23 g daily corresponding to 0·51 g/kg daily. Plasma protein levels were normal and no clinical signs of protein malnutrition were seen. These adults apparently adapt to this low protein intake which is confirmed by the extremely low blood urea level and low urinary nitrogen excretion. The question, however, we have to ask here is whether this minimal protein level should also be considered an adequate or optimal level. Although no definite answer to this question can be given, at least two reasons are in favour of the opinion that this minimal level is not the optimal one. First, the relatively frequent appearance of protein malnutrition in adult women during pregnancy and lactation in that region shows that the safety margin is very small and second, the fact that, whenever people have access to food richer in protein, they will increase their protein intake above this minimal level, is an indication that the basic human protein requirements might be somewhat higher.

Be this as it may, it should be clearly borne in mind that the protein needs of mankind in the future have not much to do with the physiological protein requirements but much more with what I would like to call the 'hedonistic' protein needs directly linked to the increased affluence.

Indeed, with increased living standards man everywhere increases his protein intake to levels that apparently exceed his physiological needs and, more important still, he switches from cheap vegetable protein to expensive animal protein consumption. The net result of this progression is that more and more vegetable crops are grown, not to feed man but to feed domestic animals with a very low efficiency (6–7% for beef and 30% for milk). In the USA for instance 91% of the plant protein produced is fed to livestock to produce 5·3 Mtonnes (Mt) of meat protein consumed. This craving for meat in the affluent societies puts an enormous strain on cereal production so that cereal reserves in the world are vanishing. In the competition for cereals and food the developing countries are on the losing side.

Because of the increased cereal prices the richer farmers in the developing countries will grow more high yield cereals at the expense of protein rich pulses and the poor farmers on the poor soils will increase cheap high energy crops (manioc) in order to get at least enough food to cover their energy needs. The average diet will therefore have the tendency to become poorer in protein among the underprivileged people. In a general way we may state that the net result of the increased affluence of a minority is the degradation of the food situation in the majority. Since there is no way short of dictatorship to reduce the 'luxusconsumption' of proteins in affluent societies and because of the increasing population pressure in most developing countries the only way to feed properly mankind in the future will be to produce more food containing an appropriate amount of protein.

THE CONCEPT OF THE FOOD CHAIN

There are essentially two ways of making more food available:

1. to shorten the food chain by using more efficiently foods of vegetable origin;
2. to synthesise nutrients by chemical or microbiological means.

The same general scheme can be applied to protein production.

Since the most important non-renewable resource in food production is fossil energy, every effort should be made to produce protein in the most efficient way. Calculations of energy requirements for protein yield show that vegetable crops are the most and livestock production the least efficient in this respect, protein biosynthesis being somewhere between.

OILSEED AND LEGUME PROTEINS

Although it has been recognised for a long time that vegetable proteins are the most economical source of protein, practical progress has been very slow in this respect. Oilseed meals were recognised as a potential new source of protein for human consumption in developing countries in the early 1950s and at the end of that decade the special processing conditions necessary to produce oilseed meals fit for human consumption from the major oilseeds were known (Altschul, 1958, 1969).

The major world oilseed crops are soya, cottonseed, peanut and sunflower. They are rich in oil and protein and after oil extraction a cheap, protein-rich meal is recovered. At first sight this seems to be a straightforward proposition. In practice, however, it is a long way from the oilseed to the dish. First, amino acid composition and protein value must be evaluated, then, antinutritional and toxicological factors such as antitryptic factors, haemagglutinines, gossypol, aflatoxins, etc., must be removed or avoided. Proper processing has to be developed for maximal oil extraction and concentration of the protein without damage to the nutritive value. Last but not least, these protein-rich ingredients must be introduced into traditional foods or transformed into new types of food (fabricated food) and find consumer acceptance.

Unfortunately it must be said that, by and large, all the efforts made so far for the increased use of oilseed proteins in human diets have met with very little success. There are many reasons for this:

oilseed meals have had an image of animal feed with the public and oilseed meal manufacturers have had no real incentive to go into the more elaborate processes necessary for human food;
the aflatoxin story stopped all projects based on peanuts for a number of years and created suspicion about oilseed meals in general;
the increased production of animal protein in the affluent countries augmented the demand for oilseed meals for animal feed purposes;
oilseed meals and their derivatives are not food in their own right but only ingredients.

The transformation of these ingredients into food can only be achieved with a sophisticated technology not generally available in developing countries.

What can we deduce for the future from these past failures? The place, during the next decade where oilseed protein will be used in substantial amounts in food, will be in the industrialised countries and not in the developing ones because acceptable products can only be produced by a sophisticated technology that is still too expensive for most developing countries. In industrial countries the *per caput* use of oilseed protein in my opinion will increase slowly but constantly and the increase will come

128   J. MAURON

almost exclusively from soya protein. In developing countries the introduction of oilseed protein into food will be slower and will generally need
some governmental support. In addition to soya, other oilseeds may have
some chances of success in developing countries such as peanut in India,
coconut in the Philippines, cottonseeds in Latin America and Mung bean
in Thailand. A new promising source of vegetable protein now grown in
New Guinea is the winged bean (*Psophocarpus tetragonolobus* L.).

LEAF PROTEIN

Green leaves are the biggest producers of protein in a plant and supply
protein to the other tissues of the plant including the seeds which are
subsequently used to nourish humans and animals. However, leafy plants
contain high concentrations of structural materials (*e.g.* cellulose, lignin)
which are largely indigestible by man. Of the leafy plants, improved forage
crops such as alfalfa constitute the most promising group as a source of a
massive amount of leaf protein concentrates (LPC). In addition there are
thousands of other leafy plants not now considered in agriculture.

For the purposes of protein isolation, however, the concentration of
protein in even young dried alfalfa is relatively low (17–25%) in comparison with oilseed meals (40–50%). It therefore seems essential for any
economically sound system for recovery of leaf protein to be based on
simultaneous production of economically valuable high quality feed from
the remainder of the plant.

The use of alfalfa as a protein source presents some toxicological
problems since it contains physiologically deleterious components (*e.g.*
saponins and oestrogen).

It may be concluded that LPC has a certain potential as a protein source
for man but will not play an important role during the next decade because
economical and safe production as well as user acceptance have not yet
been sufficiently established. It might, however, be introduced at the village
level in some developing countries.

POTATOES

Production of protein and other nutrients by the potato per hectare is as
high as any food crop in the temperate zone. Potato contains 10–12%
crude protein on a dry weight basis, although in the fresh potato about
50% of this protein occurs as available free amino acids. Thus the potato
has protein concentrations comparable with those of cereal grains but its
protein quality is much better and comparable with an animal protein.
Since it is successfully grown in warm climates for a continual supply of

fresh food, great efforts should be made to develop varieties especially suited to hot climates and to improve the protein content by genetic means. The potato is an excellent and inexpensive source of nutrients for expanding populations and its versatility makes it adaptable to a wide range of environments.

CEREAL CROPS

Cereals are not only the biggest part of the food supply but are also the largest protein source for mankind. The introduction of high yield cereal strains during the last decade has certainly been the greatest single advance in food production, although some drawbacks are now evident. Plant breeders have succeeded in developing cereal strains that are richer in protein, but generally this is done at the expense of protein quality. Geneticists have developed successful mutations in corn, barley and sorghum resulting in higher levels of lysine in the feed proteins. However, the single gene mutations involved change the proportions of the few kinds of protein that normally constitute the storage protein complement of seeds, but without apparently affecting their amino acid composition. This may be the only mechanism by which significant changes in overall amino acid composition of the seed can occur and any improvement in nutritional quality must therefore depend on changing ratios of storage protein constituents in favour of one or more nutritionally better amino acid balances. Such a mechanism is involved in the opaque-2 mutant of corn in which the nutritionally deficient zein protein fraction is drastically reduced. Similar changes account for nutritional differences found in certain barley and sorghum mutants where higher lysine levels occur with a reduction in prolamine levels.

Apparently the situation is different for rice and wheat. Rice already has a low proportion of prolamine and no prolamine depressing mutation would have much effect in altering amino acid composition. Wheat does have a sizable proportion of the total seed protein as prolamine, but mutants which cause its repression are recessive, because of the hexaploid nature of the wheat species.

At present, much basic information concerning the regulation of the storage of the products of protein synthesis in plants is still lacking and therefore it may be expected that progress will be relatively slow.

In closing this chapter on vegetable protein sources it may be interesting to look at the energy constraints on food production. The most important non-renewable resource in crop and livestock production is fossil energy. Its requirements in advanced agriculture for production of protein in various crops have been calculated (Tables 1 and 2). It is evident from these figures that even in highly advanced agriculture the energy needs for

TABLE 1

ENERGY REQUIREMENTS FOR PROTEIN PRODUCTION
Pre-industrial systems

Country	Agriculture	Crop	Energy/kg protein (MJ)	Energy ratio
Africa (averages)	Subsistence	Millet	3·8	36·2
Africa (averages)	Subsistence	Corn	4·2	37·7
Mexico	Subsistence	Corn	5·2	30·6
Tanzania	Subsistence	Rice	8·2	23·4
India	Subsistence	Rice (+ meat + milk)	11·3	14·8
Africa, Kalahari (Bushmen)	Hunters and gatherers	Nuts, vegetables, animals	11·3	7·8
Guatemala	Subsistence	Corn	11·8	13·6
Africa (averages)	Subsistence	Manioc	15·0	61·0

TABLE 2

ENERGY REQUIREMENTS FOR PROTEIN PRODUCTION
Semi- and full-industrial systems (~ 1972)

Country	Agriculture	Crop	Energy/kg protein (MJ)	Energy ratio
Philippines	Semi-industrial	Rice	33	5·51
USA	Industrial	Rice	143	1·29
UK	Industrial	Wheat	42	3·35
India	Semi-industrial	Wheat	76	1·69
Mexico	Semi-industrial	Corn	33	4·87
USA	Industrial	Corn	62	2·58
UK	Industrial	Potatoes	96	1·57
UK	Non-agricultural	SCP (methanol)	170	0·13
UK	Industrial	Milk	208	0·374
UK	Industrial	Broiler meat	290	0·10
UK	Industrial	Eggs	353	0·14
UK	Non-agricultural	Fisheries	489	0·05

protein production are many times less in vegetable crops than in animal production.

We can conclude that in the future plant crops will constitute the most important food and protein source of mankind. This is therefore an area in which the greatest research and development effort from governments and industry is justified.

BIOLOGICAL NITROGEN FIXATION

Nitrogen is vital to increase food production. The recent major escalation in the cost of nitrogen fertiliser has stimulated interest in possibilities for increasing the biological means for fixing nitrogen. This requires greater understanding of the processes involved and of the organisms that have this capacity.

The genes coding for nitrogenase in bacteria have been successfully transferred from one species to another and the genetic potential exists for extending this nitrogen-fixing ability to a variety of economically important organisms. However, research on this is still rather limited and it will take at least 10 more years to develop a process of potential agronomic significance.

PROTEIN BIOSYNTHESIS

Single cell protein (SCP) is a generic term for protein produced through fermentation of petroleum derivatives or organic wastes by single cell organisms such as yeasts, bacteria or fungi. Some forms of SCP have been used as human food for millions of years. Any fermented food will contain significant quantities of micro-organisms as diverse as bacteria, yeast and fungi. Thus there should be nothing fundamentally repugnant about eating these organisms as foods.

YEAST AND BACTERIA

The most spectacular development in the field of SCP is certainly the industrial cultivation of yeast and bacteria on n-alkanes, a fossil substrate. The pioneering work in this field was started 15 years ago at the French subsidiary of British Petroleum. Two continuous processes were finally developed, both using the same yeast (*Candida lipolitica*) as the micro-organism. In the first, yeast is grown on gas oil as the substrate and is subsequently freed from the unmetabolised hydrocarbon residues by solvent extraction and the dewaxed gas oil returns to the refinery. The alternative process uses purified *n*-alkanes as substrates so that the recovered yeast can be used directly as feedstuff. The protein value of the product is very similar to that of soya.

Another development was initiated some years later by a joint team from Exxon and Nestlé with a bacteria (*Acinetobacter*). At first *n*-alkanes were used as the substrate, and later on, ethanol. The first generation product developed consisted essentially of the dried bacteria. The second generation consisted of purified bacteria, treated to remove most of the nucleic acids. The protein value of the latter product is similar to that of casein.

Another bacterial product (*Pseudomonas*) of similar nutritive value is being developed by Imperial Chemical Industries (ICI) in England using methanol as the substrate.

Relevant composition data for these products are given in Table 3. They show essentially that the amino acid composition is fixed genetically, whereas the fatty acid distribution is determined by the substrate. Research and development on SCP production have been intense for over a decade, and as a consequence there are several large SCP plants in operation for animal feed production. However, temporary prohibition of SCP as an ingredient in animal feed by regulatory agencies in Italy and in Japan represents a serious setback for this development. This shows that the earlier enthusiasm was not justified and that a great many obstacles will have to be overcome before SCP can become a major food for man. It can be expected, however, that during the next decade there will be a considerable extension of feed yeast production on *n*-alkanes in countries where no soya is available, and this will happen in spite of economic, regulatory, and political difficulties. In the long run alkane grown yeast will help to maintain satisfactory animal protein production, without any increase in the use of arable land. It has been calculated that a 10% supplement to the world's food supply could be provided by an SCP fermentor occupying an area equivalent to about $1 \cdot 5$ km^2 of the earth's surface. It can be a truly biosynthetic yet complete source of food value whose composition can be partly controlled by the choice of micro-organisms and the composition of the medium. This is a very positive contribution from the ecological point of view.

The biggest drawback of bacteria and yeast grown on petroleum derivatives is the relatively high energy needs of the operation, which is, however, lower than that of animal protein production. A possibility of overcoming this energy drawback is the use of photosynthetic micro-organisms.

ALGAE

The advantage of algae is that they grow on inorganic substrates and directly convert sun energy into food with minimum of land use. A square

TABLE 3

EVALUATION OF SCP AMINO ACID POTENTIAL

	Yeast	Bacteria			
	Candida lipolytica	Acinetobacter anitratus			Pseudomonas
	On paraffins	On paraffins	On ethanol	On ethanol processed	On methanol
Conventional protein (%) (N × 6.25)	65·0	67·0	77·5	79·5	76·0
True protein (%)	58·5	51·5	61·0	76·5	71·5
Nucleic acid (%)	6·5	15·5	16·5	3·0	4·5
Essential amino acids (g/16g N)	43·3	35·5	36·3	48·0	43·6
Essential amino acids/total amino acids (%)	46·0	44·0	44·0	45·0	46·0
Sulphur-amino acids (g/16g N)	2·7	2·7	2·7	3·6	3·5
Lysine (g/16g N)	7·7	5·3	5·1	6·7	7·0
PER (casein=3.0)	2·5	2·0	1·9	2·9	2·6

yard of algae can actually cover the energy and nutrient needs for a man during a year. To achieve the same result with conventional agriculture 0·4 ha are needed. Different types of algae are grown for food use. Historically, it should be noted that *Spirulina maxima* was used as a staple food by the natives of lake Chad as well as by the Aztecs in Mexico. Industrial cultivation was taken up by the Institut Français du Pétrole together with a company Sosa Texcoco of Mexico in September 1972. The production so far reaches 2 tons/day. Part is used as an ingredient of biscuits and part as a poultry feed ingredient because it gives a deep yellow colour to the egg yolk.

The advantage of *Spirulina* is that it grows on an alkaline medium using nitrate as the nitrogen source. It is therefore very resistant to infections and because of the high solubility of carbon dioxide in an alkaline medium, the photosynthesis rate is very high, but even *Spirulina* cultivation under these rather good conditions is borderline economically speaking. Other projects of growing algae for food purposes are still less promising. A possible exception is the new strain of *Scenedesmus* developed at the Max Plank Institute at Dortmund. A pilot plant is in operation in Thailand and the product is being evaluated for its taste in Thailand and in Peru. Commercially, the whole venture appears still to be very uncertain. A price of 30 US cents/pound for a production of 200 tons/year has been quoted.

Chlorella was studied extensively in the 1960s in the USA, initially for feeding astronauts during space travel. *Chlorella*, however, is not of much interest because of its low digestibility and relatively poor nutritional value.

In general, we may say that algae are interesting in the sense that they do not use up much of our energy sources but convert directly sun energy into food. The protein value of algae is generally good. The limiting amino acids are the sulphur amino acids, which is the case for most micro-organisms. The prospect for use as a food is good for *Spirulina*, since it has been used traditionally by some people for centuries. For the other algae the food use is still uncertain because of gastrointestinal intolerance when consumed in large amounts. The economics of industrial algae production is still very uncertain.

CRITICAL APPRAISAL OF SCP AS HUMAN FOOD

The prospect of using SCP in food is still relatively small. Apart from some strains of algae, such as *Spirulina*, and of yeasts, such as *Saccharomyces* and *Candida* grown on conventional substrates, no SCP product studied so far can be considered absolutely safe and wholesome for man. Certainly some of the SCP products have already undergone complete chronic toxicity tests on animals successfully, but only extensive feeding tests in human beings can give final security. Indeed, several types of single cell proteins, when fed regularly to humans, have been shown to provoke gastrointestinal discomfort, sometimes with nausea, vomiting and diarrhoea, as well as allergic skin manifestations. The important point in all these experiments is, that the materials had been tested previously on animals without any detectable deleterious effects.

Preliminary results show, however, that purified bacteria, so-called second generation products, do not provoke these allergic reactions, indicating that for human consumption the whole dried micro-organism is not suitable but needs further processing to eliminate, not only nucleic acids, but other deleterious substances. In the future, at least three generations of SCP products should be envisaged (Table 4).

TABLE 4

STAGES IN THE PRODUCTION OF FOOD FROM SCP

1st generation	Crude SCP	⟶ Animal feed
	Removal of RNA	
2nd generation	Processed SCP	⟶ Limited use in foods
	Removal of cell walls	
3rd generation	SCP—protein Isolate	
	Construction	⟶ Meat analogues

First generation products are not suitable as food. They can only be used as animal feed; second generation products could eventually be envisaged for use in food but, for the time being, safety and tolerance tests in humans are not extensive enough to allow their use in food. Third generation products can be envisaged as food ingredients but not in the near future because they will have to pass all the safety and tolerance tests before their use is permitted.

We can conclude that the prospects for SCP as food during the next decade are very slim indeed.

CHEMICAL SYNTHESIS

One of the classic ways in which protein resources can be increased is the improvement of low quality protein by supplementation with the amino acid most limiting in the protein. This approach has been suggested for use on a large scale in many parts of the world to improve the quality of wheat, corn and other staple protein sources. Many studies have been performed which suggest considerable improvement of protein quality by such supplementation. The advantage of this procedure is that no change in agriculture or in cultural technology or feeding patterns is required. The cost of such supplementation is relatively low, of the order of 1–3% of the basic price of the cereal. At present amino acids are produced by fermentation and/or synthesis.

Amino acid fortification is well established in the feed industry, whereas its application in food is still relatively limited. A slow but steady increase of the latter application may be foreseen during the next decade. The synthesis of protein-like polypeptides from ammonia, water and carbon dioxide or mixtures of amino acids also appears feasible. Under a range of conditions the amino acids formed by such thermosynthesis undergo direct polymerisation during their synthesis to form 'protenoids'.

Although recent studies have demonstrated the utilisability of these products in limited feeding studies with mice, it is clear that the use of 'protenoids' cannot be envisaged for a long time to come because nothing is known about their safety and the cost of their production is absolutely prohibitive.

PRACTICAL APPLICATION OF PROTEIN SOURCES

Whereas most classic protein sources (legumes, cereals, potatoes, etc.) can each be used as a food in its own right the newer protein sources are just food ingredients but not complete foods. Nobody is eager to eat a bland, colourless and tasteless powder. The problem of transforming such ingredients into food is therefore a critical one which has not yet been completely solved.

Protein rich weaning foods
Simple mixtures of cereals with vegetable protein concentrates have been developed to be used as food supplements especially for preschool children. The archetype for this approach has been Incaparina in Central America containing maize and cottonseed flour. It was put on the market in Guatemala in 1960 and has had a mixed story of commercial failure and success in Latin America since then. More than 20 other protein rich food mixtures have reached a distribution stage but only one or two have been successful commercially.

The reasons for these failures are certainly very complex but in general it can be said that their taste was not sufficiently attractive, that they were generally considered as poor man's food and that the commercial incentives to go into this market are very meagre indeed. It appears that in a free market economy the problem cannot be solved and that in the future only joint ventures involving local governments and industry will have some chance of success.

Vegetable milk and protein beverages
There is considerable interest in extending the scarce milk supply in developing countries by diluting the cow's milk with vegetable proteins such as peanut, soya or cottonseed. Such vegetable 'toned' milk not only extends the milk supply but is actually physiologically more suitable for most non-white people in developing countries because of the widespread lactose intolerance in adults, and in children recovering from malnutrition. Complete replacement of cow's milk with vegetable milk is feasible and nutritionally sound, as shown by the prolonged and successful feeding of babies with soya milk. It is striking, however, that complete vegetable milks meant to replace cow's milk in infant feeding have been commercialised only in affluent societies for babies suffering from cow's milk allergy. These vegetable milks are more expensive than cow's milk. The commercial tendency for protein beverages is in the direction of soft drinks but the only example of outstanding commercial success is that of Vitasoy in Hong Kong, where it competes very well with the best soft drinks on the market, in spite of its soya taste. So far all attempts to introduce similar soya beverages in Latin America have failed. In these countries only beverages in which the soya taste has been completely eliminated will have a chance of success.

In the long run, however, vegetable milk products will become compulsory in most developing countries because cow's milk production will never keep pace with the population increase and the import of cow's milk products will be reduced because of a lack of foreign currency. The food industry should make a much greater effort to develop new vegetable milk products using local vegetable protein sources. Soya, peanut and coconut appear to have the greatest chances as basic raw materials.

ADVANCED OILSEED PROTEIN FOOD TECHNOLOGY

During the last 10 years considerable strides have been made in developing a more sophisticated soya protein technology. Two processes have been developed: extrusion-cooking and spinning.

The cheaper extrusion process in which the dough containing the oilseed meal is forced under high pressure through an extruder yielding textured chunks is already in commercial operation in the most advanced industrial countries. The product is used essentially as a meat extender in different ways and to a lesser extent in snacks. The alternative, more complex and more expensive process is spinning. The basic raw material in this case is a protein isolate obtained from soya. The latter is slurried in an alkaline solution and forced through a small hole into an acid-salt coagulating bath. The fibres are washed, coloured, flavoured and assembled into bundles in such a way as to simulate meat. Such products are already commercialised but only on a small scale.

What are the future trends to be expected in this dynamic field? Undoubtedly textured vegetable proteins are here to stay. In the years to come there will be a considerable increase of sales of extruded soya protein as a meat extender in the industrial countries because of the steady increase in the price of meat. The use of spun protein as meat replacer will increase only slowly. It can be anticipated that in a decade or so 10 % of all meat products will be replaced by textured vegetable protein in Anglo-Saxon countries. In continental Europe the increase will be slower but it will follow the US trend with a lag period of several years.

In developing countries only the cheaper extrusion technology can be applied to replace meat in gravies, chunky sauces, meat cubes, seasoning, etc. Extrusion products are also to be preferred in these countries because they retain the whole nutritive value of soya, whereas spun products are generally made from soya protein isolates of lower nutritive value. In India similar development could be envisaged based on groundnuts. We are developing less sophisticated, cheaper texturising processes, based on existing equipment for developing countries.

CONCLUSION

In the future there will be increased awareness that the huge reservoir of plant proteins is still not very well utilised to feed mankind and that absolute priority should be given to developing the use of these vegetable sources.

SCP should make its important contribution in this scheme in sparing valuable vegetable protein concentrates that will thus become available for food use. At the same time, SCP for animal feed will help to maintain satisfactory meat production that appears to be so important to satisfy the 'hedonistic' needs of man in affluent societies.

REFERENCES AND BIBLIOGRAPHY

Altschul, A. M. (1958). *Processed Plant Protein Foodstuffs*, Academic Press, New York.

Altschul, A. M. (1969). 'Food proteins for humans', *Chem. Eng. News*, **24**, 68–81.

Leach, G. (1975). *Energy and Food Production*, International Institute for Environment and Development, London and Washington, D.C.

Mauron, J. (1971). 'Erschliessung neuer nahrungsquellen', *Bibl. Nutr. et Dieta*, No. 16, pp. 169–191, Karger, Basel.

Mauron, J. (1973). 'Technology of protein synthesis and protein-rich foods', *Bibl. Nutr. et Dieta*, No. 18, pp. 24–44, Karger, Basel.

Mauron, J. (1975). 'Future trends in the application of new sources of protein', *Bibl. Nutr. et Dieta*, No. 21, pp. 147–162, Karger, Basel.

Scrimshaw, N. S., Wang, D. I. C. and Milner, M. (1975). *Protein Resources and Technology: Status and Research Needs—Research Recommendations and Summary*, NSF-RA-T-75-037.

PART 4

CONSTRAINTS ON MEETING THE NEEDS AND WANTS OF PEOPLE

CHAPTER 13

Families who cannot afford to feed themselves

LEONARD JOY

Institute of Development Studies, University of Sussex

The distinguishing characteristic of the malnourished is their impoverishment. It is true that there are those who could potentially so improve the management of their resources that they might feed adequately. It is even true that deterioration of diets and of nutrition status is in some cases correlated with the increase of incomes. But, while these are important qualifications which suggest that we can do something to improve nutrition among some people other than simply by improving their incomes, it is nevertheless clear that malnutrition will continue so long as there are people who are unable to subsist. The core of the world's growing problem of malnutrition is to be found among the growing numbers of people who cannot afford to subsist.

Popular presentations of the problems of malnutrition tend to focus on 'primitive' communities: on sub-Saharan nomads and shifting cultivators. They emphasise population growth, ecological imbalance and the inadequacy of primitive technologies to maintain the required increases in food production. Yet the numbers of people whose condition is appropriately described in these terms are small relative to the numbers of the malnourished who are to be found in societies which are experiencing rapid flux under the pressure of commercialisation and 'development'. Commercialisation adds to the pressure on land, since, with commerce, land is in demand to produce considerably more than the subsistence needs of foods and raw materials of those actually working it. But its enhancement as an asset is only one of the many forces at work in displacing people from the land, and precluding successive generations from cultivation rights in holdings adequate to their subsistence. With commercialisation land becomes property rather than a socially controlled community asset; new technologies encourage large scale production, or at least offer new means or inducements to the effective management of large units. New technologies, high food prices and the ready availability of casual labour destroy mutual interdependence and erode traditional patterns of rights and obligations between landlord and labourer which for centuries ensured the subsistence of the landless and near-landless. *'Development' and*

143

*population growth together are producing massive economic and social
displacement. The evidence is that wage employment and non-farm self
employment are not growing nearly fast enough to take care of the
displaced.*

The result of this process is not simply the growth of the rural poor but
also their overspill into the towns, and their emergence as urban, shanty-
town poor.

For families who cannot afford to feed themselves—rural or urban—the
most important thing to be done is to ensure their productive employment.
Development strategies need to be found which reduce displacement and
avoid those measures which increase it. But in much of the rural world the
elimination of malnutrition could be a practical reality now if community
responsibility were accepted for its reduction.

Popular presentation of the nutrition problem also tends to focus on
infant malnutrition and, indeed, among the poor, malnutrition is most
conspicuously manifest among mothers and children. However, attempts
to deal directly with this problem by providing rehabilitation to malnourished children, even when combined with simultaneous efforts to
feed and educate their mothers to good family feeding practices, typically
results in improvement followed by relapse. This is hardly surprising where
the root cause is not affected.

Malnutrition is usually only one aspect of a syndrome of ill health,
which also includes other disease conditions. Where this is the case,
improved nutrition alone will not restore and sustain health: neither will
health be restored and sustained without adequate nutrition. Usually ill
health, as a personal syndrome, is only one aspect of a more complex
social syndrome characterising the group afflicted: a consequence of their
relationship to society at large. As malnutrition needs to be treated as one
aspect of a malnutrition/ill health syndrome, so, similarly, malnutrition
and ill health need ultimately to be treated as particular aspects of a
broader social problem. Applied nutritional programmes and medical care
services alone cannot produce a healthy social environment. But neither is
a healthy social environment possible without the adequate provision of
nutrition and health services. The fact that there are limits to what such
services can achieve without more fundamental measures does not mean
that they should not be vigorously promoted.

Let us consider what health services and nutrition programmes might
achieve. For this purpose I would like to sketch out the broad features of a
'not atypical' situation. I have chosen an 'Asian-type' village situation, but,
while they may have a different flavour, many of the elements described
are to be found in other rural situations.

The situation I have in mind is characterised by heavy pressure of
population on the land. Population is still growing and inheritance patterns
are leading to the fragmentation of holdings, and the emergence of many

who do not have enough land on which to subsist. Many are landless, some are tenants who feel in danger of displacement by their landlord seeking to resume direct cultivation of the land or for other reasons. There may be considerable disparity in the production and productivity of different holdings related to the extent to which they use new seed, fertilisers, and other features of modern technology. This in turn is likely to be related to other socio-economic characteristics. A considerable amount of grain may be sold and consumed by people outside the village: perhaps 30% or more of the total production of the village. Some families will be relatively wealthy; others extremely poor, and to a large degree dependent upon gifts of food, or 'loans' in respect of which they have become indefinitely indebted. Sanitation will be generally poor, but it still may be worse for some than for others. Parasitic infestations in particular may be related to the level of living. There will be periods of the year when respiratory or gastro-intestinal diseases are common, and again, their incidence will be heaviest among the poor whose housing, clothing, heating, hygiene and diets are least adequate. Not only will poor diets predispose to infection, so also will infection lead to reduced intake and, in children, to reduced growth. Food supplies fluctuate and the availability of some food items will be highly seasonal. The poor will be least able to maintain adequate and varied diets. When there is flood or drought there may be general hardship, but again, the poorest will be the most vulnerable and they will be especially badly hit if, as a result, employment opportunities are reduced.

As the population grows and as the number of landless labourers increases, competition for jobs will become increasingly severe. An increasing number of families will find themselves unable to rely on the willingness of a patron to find work for them, for payment in grain, and they will find increasingly that they are competing for casual work paid in cash. If inflation is severe, and food prices high, food may be expensive in the village even in years of good harvest, and those who have neither land nor jobs may be badly hit. Conversely, if food prices are low, those who otherwise grow just enough surplus to meet their cash needs will have to sell more food and eat less.

In presenting this picture I have stressed the interdependence of malnutrition and disease. I have also suggested that, typically, the total food production of such a village is likely to be more than enough to ensure that nobody in that village is undernourished. Quite probably, the total amount of grain required to supplement deficient diets and ensure that the malnourished were adequately fed would amount to less than 2% of the total production of the village. Moreover, the improvement of sanitation and water supply, the provision of prenatal, perinatal and postnatal care, and of immunisation services as part of a community health programme (based on the use of auxiliaries and a routinised referral system) should not be beyond the resources of such a village, and its cost would represent a comparatively small percentage of its total production.*

But such activities would presuppose some system for taxation and redistribution of benefits, it would imply 'political will' both in the village and in support of national programmes of which the village programme would need to be a part if such a solution were to have general significance. Even with such a programme, there would be problems in ensuring that the poorest had access to the benefits of its services. Unless *communities* are willing to accept responsibility for addressing the problems of the poorest, their problems will not be addressed.

Let us assume, however, that proposals for community health services were adopted and effectively pursued. What might they hope to achieve? Sanitation and water supply improvements could reduce parasitic infestation and water-borne diseases; immunisation could control whooping cough and measles; the incidence, duration and severity of respiratory and gastro-intestinal infections could be reduced; anaemia and avitaminosis could be reduced; mothers could be encouraged into good child feeding practices within the limits of their ability to follow them in face of practical problems of hygiene, food preparation, feeding routines and the availability of recommended foods; improved child spacing might also be encouraged. These would all be tremendous achievements which should be reflected in morbidity and mortality statistics and in height and weight records, quite apart from more direct evidence of improved wellbeing and increased activity. The possibilities for such programmes should be widely explored and they should be encouraged and generally promoted.

But even if the poorest benefited from such programmes, their basic poverty would still remain. Given also the trends in displacement previously described, the numbers in such poverty would continue to increase (even more!), and at some point the costs of these redistributive measures would be reflected in some reduction of investment in increasing total production. What, ultimately, is important is that the poor should be made more productive: that they should derive some of the benefit of the total increases in productivity of the community. Thus, at base, there are key problems of employment, of land policy and settlement, and of the productivity of marginal holdings. A failure to identify and implement rural programmes which are effective in these respects—in making the poor productive while raising total output—will mean both rural and urban poverty and malnutrition must grow.

In the past, it was believed that the elimination of poverty presupposed the achievement of fairly high national incomes. This presumption needs

---

* An example of such a community health programme and its costs is given in WHO *Health By the People* (Geneva, 1975) in the article by Mabelle Arole and Rajanikant Arole, 'A comprehensive rural health project in Jamkhed (India)'.

to be questioned. It needs to be questioned especially because it is now clear that the development process itself actually aggravates poverty and malnutrition. What we need to explore is the extent to which, by concerning ourselves with the welfare of families who cannot afford to feed themselves, we can substantially alleviate, and even reduce poverty, without prejudice to sustained increases in material output. Such an approach would require a considerable reorientation in planning procedures, but it may be essential if malnutrition is to be reduced. Simply increasing food production and providing for government-operated, taxation- or inflation-financed nutrition programmes will not solve the problem.

It would be foolish to argue that increased availability of food could not allow, or even directly result in, the reduction of malnutrition. But the manner by which food supplies are increased rather than the quantity of their increase may be what most determines the impact on malnutrition. The fall in the price of grain consequent on an increase in supply will be little compensation to the undernourished town labourer who has been displaced from his rural livelihood by the very measures which increased the supply. This is not to argue that supplies should not be increased, but to argue that the net effects of the specific measures used to increase supply should be assessed. It is not to argue either that measures are never justified which aggravate malnutrition among some people; it does argue, however, that there should be concern for complementary measures to support those who suffer in the name of some greater good.

Ultimately, policies aimed at generating increased production must break down because nobody will produce food for those who cannot afford to pay. My earlier discussion on community approaches presupposed that payment would be made out of taxes or inflationary deficit financing. We know that few governments will be able to sustain such measures—politically or economically.

Nowadays, we are much concerned about the ability of the world to feed itself. This amounts, in effect, for the present at any rate, to a concern that the world will not pay the cost of increasing production to the level sufficient to meet the needs of the undernourished as well as the demands of the well nourished. The problem is primarily one of how to ensure that the demands of the needy are made effective. Clearly, new methods of production which reduce costs per unit of output improve the potential for ensuring that all are adequately fed. But, depending on the technology required to reduce production costs, such innovations might bring home very starkly the fact that ultimately the solution to malnutrition is social rather than technological. This point will be clear from a hypothetical illustration. Suppose that a new variety of rice were developed which could be sown broadcast (and not transplanted as is generally the case at present) and that a cheap herbicide greatly reduced cultivation and weeding costs. Even were such a new variety to have double the yields of current varieties, one immediate impact in, say, Bengal, would be the massive displacement of many people who are now critically dependent on seasonal employment in rice cultivation and transplanting. If such innovations were compounded by the use of simple seeders to ensure even crop stands and high plant populations, and by simple mechanical harvesters and threshers, then we would surely have a recipe for mass malnutrition and maybe for revolution. This is not to argue, of course, that such innovations are undesirable and are not to be sought. But it does argue that for technical change to be socially desirable overall, there may need also to be an accompanying social change.

The problem that the world is faced with at present is precisely a problem of social change: a problem that society has not effectively addressed itself to in most parts of the world. For the most part we seek solutions in further technical innovation, but the reality we must face is that in some degree the solution must involve social innovation. Moreover, to a large extent the problem could be solved now by appropriate social action and without new technology. I make this point with considerable emphasis, because I believe that it is important that an understanding of it should be reflected in these proceedings. We would be wrong to examine the contribution of technology to the solution of nutrition problems without a balanced and integrated consideration of the social context in which technology must be developed and applied.

The constraint on families who cannot afford to feed themselves is their low productivity. The solution to the core of the world's malnutrition problem lies in making the poor productive. This does *not* mean making yet greater efforts to promote economic development. It means devising ways—specific concrete ways for specific poor people—of absorbing people in creative employment and in making their employment more productive. This is partly a matter of development strategy. But it is mostly a matter of asking in each village and each district 'who are the people giving cause for concern?' 'in what ways might *they* be productively absorbed?' 'in what ways can *their* output be increased?' In some places where the ecology is harsh it will not be easy to find answers to these questions. But in others it will be readily possible to see what might be done to absorb people in developing and exploiting natural resources. There will be problems in getting planners to ask the right questions and to consider answers which involve social innovation or political resistance. If they do come up with such answers the problem will be one of carrying them through. Clearly political commitment is a precondition. But commitment requires the acceptance of the implications of alternative courses of action based on an understanding of what these truly are. It is important that we should project a correct picture of the alternatives and their implications.

CHAPTER 14

Problems of interdependence— is food a special case?

GEORGE HOUSTON

University of Glasgow

'The capital employed in agriculture ... not only puts into motion a greater quantity of productive labour than any equal capital employed in manufacturing but in proportion, too, to the quantity of productive labour which it employs, it adds a much greater value ... to the real wealth and revenue of its inhabitants. Of all the ways in which a capital can be employed, it is by far the most advantageous to the society.'
'When by the improvement and cultivation of land the labour of one family can provide food for two, the labour of half the society becomes sufficient to provide food for the whole.'

(From Adam Smith, *The Wealth of Nations*, 1776.)

I have chosen these quotations from the *Wealth of Nations* not only because this year marks the bicentenary of its publication (an occasion in which Glasgow University has a strong interest) but because they illustrate that the conflicting influences now affecting agriculture have a long recorded history. Adam Smith, although rejecting the physiocratic view that only agriculture was productive, was still an agricultural fundamentalist in that he gave agriculture precedence over manufacture or trade. At the same time he recognised that with the economic progress of society there was bound to be a decline in the proportion of people engaged in food production.

Smith's arguments for giving agriculture precedence are not without ambiguity. But if we interpret them as meaning that in the 18th century a given additional investment in agriculture would have led to a greater increase in employment and a greater increase in the value of output than would be obtained elsewhere, then we would all be anxious to see more of the arguments and evidence on which this view was based. The 200 years which have elapsed have been characterised by a relative and absolute decline in agricultural employment in Britain and a relative decline (though absolute increase) in the value of farm output. It can be argued that the decline in the economic role of agriculture has at certain times been too rapid but it would be difficult to sustain the view that over the

149

period as a whole the shift of investment resources into non-agricultural sectors has not been a necessary condition of our improved economic conditions. As the second quotation from Smith implies, the human demand for food has not so far grown at the same rate as our technical ability to increase its production.

Probably the best known propositions of the *Wealth of Nations* concern not agriculture but the division of labour, its contribution to productivity and its limitation by the extent of the available markets. Adam Smith may have been an agricultural fundamentalist in the sense already indicated, but he was no believer in self sufficient economic communities; on the contrary he was an exponent of the various virtues of interdependence, an advocate of specialisation and of the freedom of trade required to enable it to flourish.

Whether Smith's views on such matters always avoided inconsistencies is not strictly relevant to the theme of this paper. But it is pertinent to note that the real economic conditions of society in his day produced an agricultural dilemma which has never disappeared. Agriculture, in an obvious and practical sense, is uniquely fundamental to human existence, yet its relative decline has been an essential feature of economic progress. To neglect it would bring disaster, to protect it from (relative) contraction would ensure stagnation.

The history of British agriculture and of successive governments' attitudes towards it reflect these contradictory roles. Out of all advanced industrial countries we have been most prepared to rely for our food supplies on the dynamic advantages of interdependence rather than on the security of self sufficiency. We have paid more attention to Smith's dictum on enlarging the extent of our markets than his view that agricultural investment was the most advantageous to society. Only in war time or when our international economic position was gravely threatened have we felt that the consequences of interdependence for agriculture were bad enough to justify a reversal of policies based on the general gains expected from that interdependence.

The question we now have to ask is whether—either at the world level, or in relation to Britain's own economic position—we should in the future pursue economic policies which imply still greater extensions of economic interdependence or whether we should exempt food production from this approach, if not completely, then to a greater degree than has recently been the case.

The advantages which might be expected to follow from greater interdependence between nations go beyond the standard economic benefits of comparative advantage, specialisation and trade. Better understanding, greater cultural and social contacts, mutual interest in avoiding war and reducing national prejudices—all are possible consequences as well as desirable objectives which should be pursued universally and consistently.

But all nations must determine their policies in an imperfect world whose economic and political development is far from stable. Even if we are optimists, perceiving and supporting a long term improvement in the human condition, we cannot ignore the fluctuations nor remain indifferent to our vulnerability to their effects. The greatest economic danger for any individual country is likely to come from a serious lack of balance in its international position rather than from its conformity to a general deficiency of performance. I propose to concentrate mainly on the issues affecting this country.

Britain's chronic imbalance is its very much higher dependence on imported food—no other large industrial country has to rely on foreign supplies for anything like our figure of 45%. The case for reducing that degree of dependence does not rest on a general argument for raising all countries' level of self sufficiency—that is a separate question with much wider implications. It rests on the view that Britain's economy is now specially vulnerable to certain developments and these are significantly related to our food policies.

The new aspects of our situation which greatly strengthen the case for agricultural expansion in Britain can be considered under three headings: world influences, the implications of European Economic Community (EEC) membership, and trends within Britain. At a world level, the dramatic changes since 1972 in prices and stocks have exposed the instability of the world market and its unreliability as a source of supply for basic foods. Whereas from 1950 to 1972 the world prices of food and manufactured goods had, in the long run, tended to move in line with each other, from 1972 to 1974 the price of food in world trade rose by about 35% compared with only 19% for manufactures. At the same time world stocks of many foods were severely reduced and the US government's decision to abandon its traditional stock holding role for certain products added to the uncertainty. Here in Britain our import bill for food and feed rose by £1500 million to over £3700 million, and this despite a small decline in the volume of such imports.

Changes in the terms of world trade between farm and manufactured products have occurred in the past, however, and no one can be certain that the present relationships will become firmly established. World (and UK) opinion has hardened on two crucial propositions. The first is that the balance of power in world food trade is shifting significantly from importing to exporting countries. Given the small proportion of total food production which enters world trade and the much lower proportion of trade supplies now held in reserve stocks, fluctuations in production caused by the weather or disease are likely to bring volatile conditions to world food markets. At the same time it seems unlikely that exporting countries will be as willing as in the past to allow their export prices to remain below the level of their production costs in periods of greater supply. Quite apart from the EEC, importing countries like Britain may have to suffer the consequences of periodic shortages without benefiting as much as in the past from occasional surpluses. In addition, many countries exporting basic agricultural commodities have not been slow to draw conclusions from the activities of the Organisation of Petroleum Exporting Countries (OPEC). While there are several reasons why international cartels will be more difficult to organise for commodities other than oil, the less developed (and largely agricultural) countries of the world have greatly increased their political and economic influence in world affairs and are more conscious of the possible advantages of coordinated actions in commodity trade.

The second proposition is that food deficits in parts of the less developed world are rising and leading to an increase in the import requirements of these countries. One estimate, by FAO (1975) suggests that the (theoretical) deficit in cereals alone in what are termed the developing market economies could rise to over 85 million tons by the mid 1980s compared with 16 million tons in 1969–1971 and net exports in earlier periods. The deficits are described as 'theoretical' because they rest on certain assumptions including no price changes; in practice, price rises would take place with consequent effects on demand and supply. Underlying trends of this order, even if allowance is made for the imprecise nature of such projections, will obviously have a serious impact on cereal importing countries like Britain.

To sum up, the balance of opinion on the future world food situation has moved against the view that we will soon return permanently to the price relationships of the 1950s and 1960s and to a situation where Britain could buy imported supplies at prices related to (or even lower than) the cost of production on the most efficient farms in the world. It has to be admitted, however, that economists' predictions of future world trends are rarely unanimous and even a consensus view does not merit much shorter odds than average. The new factor in the UK's situation which provides a much more reliable basis for arguing that our food procurement policies must change is our membership of the EEC and our acceptance of the basic principles of its Common Agricultural Policy (CAP), namely the establishment of common prices, internal free trade and a common system of preferences for most temperate food products. The implication of this is that in the future our agriculture will have to compete with relatively high cost European farming rather than with lower cost farming in the rest of the world, whereas many of our industries will have to face even keener competition from some of their most efficient rivals.

The main point can be made in a simplified way. Before our entry to the EEC, an increase in agricultural output in Britain had to be economically justified by showing that the resources used in producing this increase would not have been able to produce non-farm goods which could have been exchanged for a larger amount of equivalent foodstuffs on the world market. Now we have to carry out the same calculation in relation to the EEC market in which the ratio of farm to non-farm prices tends to be higher than in the world as a whole. There is little doubt that once farm product prices in Britain are brought up to the level of EEC prices (which should happen by 1978) it will be possible for sectors of our agriculture to keep expanding and still hold their costs below the EEC price level. Obviously this must be a gradual process with the expansion rate varying in different sectors. But unless there is a radical change in the CAP the case for the expansion of British agriculture is likely to remain powerful at least until we are about 90–95% self sufficient in temperate food products. Even if there is a gradual relative decline in EEC farm prices (an objective which is likely to unite German and British interests within the community) many UK farmers will be much better placed than most of their European colleagues to withstand such pressures—especially if the industry uses the more profitable years to improve its grass-based livestock enterprises.

Responsibility for any serious doubts about the future effects of the CAP must be laid at the door of the politician not the economist. At present, for example, the principle of 'common farm prices' is not applied universally, even among the original six. Variations in exchange rates (especially the revaluation of the Deutschmark) have forced the Commission to accept the need for different national farm price levels—for a temporary period at least. The UK government is not likely to be pushing very strongly for the condemnation of such heresies for they have enabled us to avoid the consequences of even higher food prices although they have also (presumably temporarily) held back the drive for agricultural expansion which is so obviously in the national interest.

Not all policy makers' weapons are as crude as the Green Pound or the 'Black' Mark. More sophisticated and less obvious ways of bending the CAP to suit national interests are likely to be used and some of these may well hinder British agriculture in adjusting optimally to EEC conditions. The dairy sector is one example. Given the increases in producers' and consumers' prices which would follow on full adoption of CAP rules, the British dairy industry could be expanded economically to a level where we were more or less self sufficient in liquid milk and dairy products. But this would mean that, at current price/cost relationships, excess supplies would probably build up in the surplus EEC countries while British farmers' output was rising and UK consumption falling (because of higher retail prices). Since the seasonal pattern of milk production differs between the UK and the surplus EEC countries, arguments about winter and summer price differentials (and quota-based price adjustments) could be a thinly disguised battle for that part of the UK dairy products market which has been traditionally supplied by low cost imported supplies. It would, however, be a political battle; on economic grounds alone the British dairy farmer would win.

The third and final aspect of what was earlier called the 'new situation' facing food producers in Britain relates to developments within the UK economy itself. Some of these can be considered to be problems of interdependence in that they have international causes or consequences but they can be distinguished from the wider world trends or EEC influences already discussed.

The relatively slow growth of the UK economy and the virtual stabilisation of our population has contributed towards our declining share of world trade in food. More than ever before we have become price takers on the world market, with little power to influence the cost of the imports we must procure to survive. Our rate of inflation and the (not unrelated) rate of depreciation of our currency have also been out of line with most of our competitors. As sterling falls on the world money market so the cost of our food imports rises and the comparative advantage of our agriculture (compared with exporting industries) improves. Last year's White Paper, *Food from Our Own Resources*, estimated that each 1 % fall in the value of sterling could add £35 million to our bill for food imports.

Against this rather depressing backdrop of the UK economy, the performance of agriculture is impressive. Over the past 10 years net output per man has nearly doubled, the rise of around 6% per annum being effected by an annual rate of growth in net output of about $2\frac{1}{2}$% and an annual decline in manpower (workers and farmers) of just over 3%. Additional agricultural investment in real resources was not too high to devalue this performance significantly and by any criteria the efficiency of the industry rose at a rate that would have been acceptable in many other sectors of the economy. At the same time the variation in technical performance (and costs of production) within British agriculture is a well known phenomenon; while uniformity is an impractical objective the extent of the present variations suggests that, even without further technical innovations, there is scope for still greater improvements in productivity. The research and development and advisory expertise available is further support for the view that the technical and economic advance of British farming need not be slowed down; on the contrary, greater economic confidence should help to maintain it close to the best rates achieved in the postwar period.

You will appreciate that in relation to British agriculture I am an unrepentant expansionist and a cautious optimist. I see no serious conflict between such an approach and a recognition and acceptance of the high degree of economic, political and cultural interdependence which we already have on a world scale. Changes in our methods of procuring and securing food supplies up to the levels I have indicated seem to me to be inevitable. Contrary to what is sometimes suggested they do not in my view conflict with any commitments we should make to the less developed countries of the world. It is not mainly cereals, meat, milk and other temperate products they wish to sell. Moreover, there is strong evidence that as a group they will be most affected by future food shortages. If the world community, in the year 2000, is faced with a problem of widespread food surpluses then it will be a legacy which I for one will be pleased to have left.

The case for producing more food in Britain does not therefore depend on our rejecting the gains from interdependence, it rests on the kind of evidence at a world, European and UK level that I have presented here and which I hope will go some way to convince you that even if Adam Smith's advice was wrong for much of the past 200 years it is not likely to be so far out in the future when the resources employed in our agriculture may well be 'the most advantageous to society'.

REFERENCES

FAO (1975). *Population, Food Supply and Agricultural Development.* (Also published as Chapter 3 of *The State of Food and Agriculture* 1974, ROME, FAO, 1975.)

Ministry of Agriculture, Fisheries and Food (1975). *Food from Our Own Resources,* Cmnd 6020, HMSO, London.

CHAPTER 15

Physical limitations on the food supply

N. W. PIRIE

Rothamsted Experimental Station, Harpenden

For the forseeable future, political and psychological factors will be more important restraints on the food supply than physical factors such as the farmed area, water, light, plant nutrients, photosynthetic efficiency, harvest ratio, and losses entailed in different methods of using crops. The more important restraints operate at all social levels: chronically semi-starved people do not envisage the possibility of better nutrition and so do not strive for it; well fed planners cannot envisage an agricultural system operating on unfamiliar processes and principles. Even if these psychological barriers can be overcome, we will not get an adequate food supply until we get rid of the political assumption that those working on the dirty side of the farm gate should be paid less than the average for the community.

THE LAND AREA

About 1·4 Ghectare (Gha) are now being cultivated. Buringh, *et al.* (1975) divided the world into 222 zones and, after considering the climate and soil characteristics of each, concluded that 3·4 Gha were potentially arable. In reaching that conclusion they did not assume that desalinated sea water would be used for irrigation, or that land would be managed in unconventional ways. Other authorities do not think the potential arable area is quite so large, but it is clear that there is still much underused land. The potentialities of the 1·5 Gha of land in the wet tropics is the main point of disagreement. Some pessimists say that that land would quickly erode if farmed conventionally; the US President's Science Advisory Committee (1967) argued that much of this soil is no worse than that of Florida 50 years ago. The disagreement illustrates a point that is too often forgotten—good farmland is usually created by skilled farming. The cost of bringing underused land into a fit state for farming would be between 200 and 3000 dollars/hectare; Buringh, *et al.* (1975) estimate that 0·9 Gha comes at the expensive end of their scale. However, two or three families can be maintained on a properly farmed hectare: the cost of establishing one work place in modern industry is more than 3000 dollars.

THE WATER AREA

Photosynthesis in the oceans is thought to produce 70 Gtonnes (Gt) of organic matter (dry weight) annually—that is 18 t per head of the world population. In most of the ocean, production is limited by lack of nitrogen and phosphorus. Most fish are therefore caught in coastal waters where rivers supply these elements, or in regions where phosphorus-rich water rises. These upwelling areas amount to only 0·1% of the 35 Gha of ocean. It is unrealistic to think of fertilising the open ocean because the fertiliser would spread into the useless unlit depths. There are, however, great potentialities in fertilising and 'farming' coastal lagoons; in South East Asia the potential area is two million hectares (Idyll, 1972), in the world as a whole the area is probably five times this.

After a period of euphoria in which oceanic resources were assumed to be almost limitless, sober opinion now puts the sustainable annual yield of conventional fish at about 100 Mt, *i.e.* less than twice the present catch. Mussels and other shellfish can be 'farmed'. When protected from predation, annual protein yields as great as 40 t/ha are claimed (Mason, 1972). Sites must be chosen carefully, for such a yield depends on products of photosynthesis, including the 1000 Gt of detritus suspended in the ocean, being brought to the molluscs by currents. Now that folly has so depleted the whale population that the catch is only a quarter of that which would be sustainable, an annual harvest of 200 Mt (wet weight) of krill could be taken (PAG, 1974). It will take time to exploit all these resources; the food supply could be increased more quickly if we ate more of the fish already caught instead of turning 36% of it into animal feed (Burgess, 1975).

IRRIGATION WATER

The distribution of water in the world is by no means ideal for agriculture. The ocean contains 95%, and 4% is frozen. Of the remaining 1%, 98·5% is underground, 1% in lakes, 0·2% in soil and 0·1% in rivers. Irrigation with river water is often easy, and becomes easier still when the river is dammed for hydro-electric power. Pumping is necessary when lake or underground water is used. The regions that most need irrigation are often windy and always sunny: serious work on wind and solar powered pumps is urgently needed. Between 10 and 15% of arable land is now irrigated—though sometimes not very efficiently. Buringh, *et al.* (1975) argue that 10–15% of the 2 Gha of unused potentially arable land will also be irrigated. This part of their argument is dubious because it is reasonable to assume that the best sites are already irrigated and that more power, and therefore expense, will be involved in irrigating new land. Excessive irrigation wastes water, but drip irrigation and similar economical methods have ruined land through salinisation. Overgrazing is an important cause of desert encroachment on arable land. More land is probably being lost in these ways than is coming into use through extended irrigation. With luck, grazing will be controlled before tsetse fly is eliminated, otherwise another million hectares will probably be ruined. Irrigation often allows two or three crops to be grown in a year in the tropics; this advantage is offset by the increased hazard from schistosomiasis and from pests which no longer die during fallow periods.

LIGHT

Artificial light is unlikely to increase world food supply by as much as 1%. Any increase would result from such processes as raising seedlings in artificial light for transplanting on to a larger area when the weather is warm. With little prospect of increasing the amount of light, what we get must be used efficiently.

The first step, obviously, is to ensure that as little light as possible escapes interception by a functional leaf. Hence transplanting, which enables land to be used by one crop while the crop that will follow it is going through the first stages of growth; and intercropping, which uses the space between slow growing plants that will ultimately become large and intercept all the light. This form of intercropping is unquestionably advantageous and should be distinguished from the cultivation of two or more species growing together at similar rates. The latter technique is probably advantageous (Trenbath, 1974)—but it complicates harvesting.

The efficiency of photosynthesis diminishes as illumination increases. The more productive crops have a vertical arrangement of their leaves so that leaf area may be 6–9 times the ground area with little mutual shading. To a great extent, the superiority of modern plant varieties depends on this 'light absorption in depth'; per unit leaf area they photosynthesise little better than primitive varieties.

The rates of photosynthesis of those agriculturally important plants that have been studied are similar in dull weather; but in sunlight, potatoes, sugar beet and wheat are less efficient than maize, sorghum, sugar cane and many tropical grasses. The group that uses strong light efficiently tends also to be more economical of water. If water and other nutrients are amply provided, if 'light absorption in depth' is catching 95% of the light on healthy green surfaces covering the whole ground surface, the theoretical limit of daily productivity is about 1 t/ha. The observed limit is 0·4–0·6 and that rate is not maintained for more than a few weeks because plants get less efficient as they mature. In the tropics, annual dry matter (DM) yields can reach 70 t/ha and 100 has been claimed. The limit in Britain is 25.

CHEMICAL INPUTS

Most of the water that a plant needs passes through it. During the period of maximum photosynthesis, most of the carbon dioxide stays inside and is the basis of the accumulation of DM. Except on very still sunny days, photosynthesis does not diminish the local supply of atmospheric carbon dioxide, but the rate can usually be enhanced by increasing the concentration of carbon dioxide in the ambient air. Many plants, especially those that use strong light efficiently, become more efficient if the concentration of oxygen is diminished. These phenomena are physiologically interesting, but it is unlikely that manipulating atmospheric composition will soon be part of large scale agriculture.

The response curve of a crop to the three main fertilisers, nitrogen, phosphorus and potassium (NPK) has the familiar 'law of diminishing returns' form. Ideally, a farmer puts on fertiliser until the extra amount costs as much as the extra yield is worth. Practically, the farmer may not get credit to buy fertiliser, and may be unwilling to buy the optimum amount if there is a chance that drought will destroy the crop. Nevertheless, it is obvious from the 'law of diminishing returns' that fertiliser will have most effect on world food supply if it is used in those regions where least is now used. There, the extra weight of crop may be 20 times the weight of fertiliser. Unfortunately, it may cost as much to get the fertiliser to such a region as to make the fertiliser.

Atmospheric nitrogen is inexhaustible because it is recycled. About 1000 Mt of nitrogen is 'fixed' annually by biological processes, the ocean contains nearly a thousand times as much, rain and industrial 'fixation' each supply 40–50 Mt annually. Provided power is available there is no limit to the amount that could be 'fixed'. However, as things stand, agriculture is likely to depend increasingly on biological fixation by symbiotic micro-organisms on the roots of legumes and, as has recently been discovered (von Bulow and Dobereiner, 1975), on some varieties of maize and other tropical grasses.

Phosphorus is more of a problem. Much of what we use goes wastefully into the ocean which already contains 100 Gt, but it is inconveniently dilute. Rock of mineable grade is thought to contain 30 Gt; we use about 13 Mt annually. The position is sufficiently alarming to make it advisable to restrict the amount of phosphorus wasted in detergents, etc., but it is not so alarming as some 'doomsters' have claimed. They overlook the fact that most of the phosphorus applied to farmland is sequestrated in the soil and is then slowly released to benefit crops for many years. Potassium is slowly leached from clay; oceanic potassium is abundant and could, with a little effort, be extracted.

A great deal of the NPK used in agriculture ends up in sewage and dung. In primitive agriculture these elements are to a large extent conserved: in sophisticated agriculture they are often expensively hurried out to sea. By ensuring that there is adequate arable land near installations where animals are kept, the waste of dung could be avoided (Table 1). Changes in this direction are inevitable and might as well be started before increased fertiliser prices force change upon us. It will be difficult to use sewage fully

TABLE 1

THE CAPACITY OF FARMLAND TO USE EXCRETIONS

One hectare of farmland can use annually 200–400 kg N
This quantity is excreted by:

3–6	dairy cows
6–10	beef animals
10–20	pigs
50–100	people
300–600	laying hens
500–1 000	broilers

The annual excretion of UK livestock is about 1 Mt N, 0·2 Mt P, 1 Mt K

because of the extent to which it is contaminated by metals such as chromium, nickel and zinc. A return to the traditional careful recycling of excreta is a sensible facet of the new cult of 'organic farming'; another facet, the deliberate growing of crops for compost, is less sensible. The phosphorus and potassium in the crop are simply being restored to the land from which they were taken; much of the carbon and nitrogen is lost through oxidation and denitrification. This is especially true when soil temperatures are high (Newton, 1960).

THE HARVEST INDEX

The abundant production of DM is not the same as the production of food—it is not even the same as the production of fodder. A few leafy vegetables such as chinese cabbage and spinach, in which nearly everything above ground is eaten, come at one extreme; that is why the cultivation of green vegetables is the most productive method of using land (Pirie, 1975a). Some of the more dramatic values are given in Table 2. The values for the three tropical vegetables would be attainable in practice in suitable climates. The value for leeks in Britain is obviously an unreal extrapolation. At the other extreme come plants such as corncockle, *Tidestromia* in Death Valley, and *Spartina* on salt marshes, which perform photosynthetic prodigies but for which nutritional roles have not yet been found. Agricultural crops are intermediate, with harvest indexes (% of the total DM that is useful) ranging from 5 to 60. Improvement is sought both by increasing the index and by using what has hitherto been wasted.

Plant breeders have been remarkably successful in diverting more of the products of photosynthesis into useful parts of the plant. Critics stress the genetic uniformity, and hence risk from disease, of short-strawed wheat,

TABLE 2

LEAFY VEGETABLES GIVING LARGE PROTEIN YIELDS

Species	Measured DM yield (Tons)	(Days)	%N	Calculated annual protein yields[a] (t/ha)
Allium porrum (leek)	6·0	84	4·8	6·0
Amaranthus cruentus	5·0	70	5·3	6·2
Brassica juncea	4·7	56	3·7	5·7
Solanum melanocerasum	3·0	70	6·7	5·2

[a] Assuming that four fifths of the N is protein and that the yield could be maintained for a year.

and the susceptibility to drought of sorghums with a harvest index of 40 instead of the traditional 7–10. But selection is in its infancy. No physiological canon forbids the presence of all the good qualities in the same variety. Physiology does, however, make it likely that photosynthesis will be most active when there is an adequate 'sink' into which the product can go. That is why potatoes and sugar beet, in which leaf and root growth proceed together, outyield sweet potato in which leaves are failing when tuber growth is starting. It is unlikely that abundant agricultural by-products will be eliminated: they should therefore be efficiently used.

CROP FRACTIONATION

All products of arable land need some form of fractionation—hence the harvest index. Traditional fractionations, such as threshing, peeling, and discarding outside leaves of vegetables need no comment. Other crops need more sophisticated treatments, some of which are traditional. Thus soya beans were fermented to improve flavour and digestibility, or their protein was extracted and coagulated. They are now often heated, or extracted protein is processed into a felt (textured vegetable protein).

Attempts are made to mechanise the traditional technique of grating fresh coconuts in warm water so that a protein and oil emulsion can be pressed out. Several other seeds are being treated in similar ways. To get maximum DM from a field it should be kept in the green, photosynthetically active, vegetative state. Photosynthesis declines as seeds ripen. The yield of protein, edible by people and other non-ruminants, is therefore greater when it is extracted from optimally manured forage crops, than when any other agricultural system is used. About a third of the protein remains in the fibrous part of the leaf for use as ruminant fodder. So much water is pressed out during the extraction that drying this residue for winter feed needs a third or less of the fuel needed to dry the original crop (Pirie, 1966). Protein can also be extracted from by-product leaves that are now wasted: in Britain, potato haulm could yield 50 000 t (Pirie, 1976; Carruthers and Pirie, 1975), and sugar beet about the same amount. The extraction procedure is discussed elsewhere (Pirie, 1971; 1975b).

CONVERSION

Conversions always involve loss; separations (*e.g.* of leaf protein) are preferable because in them there is less loss. During conversion by an animal, the loss is 70–95% (Large, 1973). This must be accepted when, as with marine fish, and cattle grazing and browsing on rough ground, there is no other feasible method of using what is eaten. Animal conversion of the whole crop from arable land is unacceptable when food becomes scarce, but many farm and urban wastes (bagasse, haulms, straw, waste paper) are, or could be turned into, ruminant feed, while wastes from food-factory and kitchen are pig and poultry food. Pigs are fed entirely on such scraps in China, and there are four times as many there as in USA—but they do not grow as fast (Sprague, 1975). Although animal products will probably become less abundant, they will not disappear.

The replacement of animals by fermentation tanks is unlikely. Micro-organisms undoubtedly give a larger return of useable product than animals, but the process is more difficult to control. A ruminant is a self reproducing, mobile, fermentation tank with automatic temperature and pH control; its size is well adapted to farm work. The thought of collecting the material that makes up half the fodder used by ruminants in Britain, and bringing it to fermentation complexes, is intimidating. The cultivation of micro-organisms on petroleum and products derived from coal involves even more sophisticated technology than their cultivation on agricultural by-products. It is therefore unlikely to have much impact on the diets of those most in need of more food. This development is, however, useful because it will increase the prestige of micro-organisms and will therefore make their cultivation on local by-products more likely.

164   N. W. PIRIE

SYNTHESIS

The limiting factor in food production is the supply of carbon in a reduced form. That is why coal and oil are possible sources. The main source is carbon reduced by photosynthesis. However, that depends on atmospheric carbon dioxide: this as Table 3 shows is one of the least abundant sources,

TABLE 3

MASS OF CARBON IN VARIOUS FORMS ON
EACH SQUARE METRE OF TOTAL WORLD
SURFACE, *i.e.* 5×10^{14} m^2

Reduced carbon	
Methane	40·0 g
Petroleum	140·0 g
Oceanic sediment	1·9 kg
Soil organic matter	2·9 kg
Oceanic water	5·4 kg
Coal, lignite, etc.	10·0 kg
Kerogen in rock	5·0 t
Oxidised carbon	
Atmospheric CO_2	1·1 kg
Oceanic CO_2	70·0 kg
Limestone and dolomite	18·0 t

though it is replenished. If energy should become abundant, food synthesis from limestone will be feasible. In present circumstances, synthesis is likely to be restricted to nutrients needed in small amounts only, *e.g.* vitamins. For our bulk foods we will depend on photosynthesis for many years.

REFERENCES

Bulow, von, J. W. W. and Dobereiner, J. (1975). *Proc. nat. Acad. Sci. USA*, **72**, 2389.
Burgess, G. H. O. (1975). In *Food Protein Sources*, edited by N. W. Pirie, Cambridge University Press, London.
Buringh, P., van Heemst, H. D. J. and Staring, G. J. (1975). Publ. 598 Landbouwhogeschool, Wageningen.
Carruthers, I. B. and Pirie, N. W. (1975). *Biotechnology and Bioengineering*, **17**, 1775.
Idyll, C. P. (1972). *Ceres*, **5**, (4), 43.

Large, R. V. (1973). In *The Biological Efficiency of Protein Production*, p. 183. Edited by J. G. W. Jones, Cambridge University Press, London.

Mason, J. (1972). *Oceanogr. Mar. Biol. Ann. Rev.*, **10**, 437.

Newton, K. (1960). *Papua and New Guinea Ag. J.*, **13**, 81.

Pirie, N. W. (1966). *Fertil. Feed. Stuffs J.*, **63**, 119.

Pirie, N. W., editor (1971). *Leaf Protein: Its Agronomy, Preparation, Quality and Use*, International Biological Program Handbook 20.

Pirie, N. W. (1975a). *Baroda J. Nutr.*, **2**, 43.

Pirie, N. W. (1975b). In *Protein Nutritional Quality of Foods and Feeds*, p. 341. Edited by M. Friedman, Marcel Dekker, New York.

Pirie, N. W. (1976). In *Food from waste*, p. 180. Edited by G. G. Birch, K. J. Parker and J. T. Worgan, Applied Science Publishers, London.

Protein Advisory Group (1974). *PAG Bulletin*, **4**, No. 2, United Nations, New York.

Sprague, G. F. (1975). *Science*, **188**, 549.

Trenbath, B. R. (1974). *Adv. Agron.*, **26**, 177.

US Pres. Sci. Adv. Com. (1967). *The World Food Problem*, US Govt. Printing Off., Washington, D.C.

Index

167